Cont[ents]

Page 2 – *Cornucopia* by Terrance Gutb[...]

Page 16 – *Funhouse* by Michael Tager

Page 26 – *The Jar Tree* by MK Sauer

Page 41 – *Humpington Plantation: A Satire* by Mike Crumplar

Page 45 – *Van Gogh's Slice* by Taryn L. Hook

Page 66 – *Before The Clock Strikes Six* by Justin Tate

Page 79 – *A Nice Guy* by R.B. Roth

Page 95 – *Wednesday's Child* by Jon Michael Kelley

Page 105 – *The Job That Needed Doing* by Jack Granath

Page 113 – *Removal* by Elizabeth Dadabo

Page 122 – *Impala* by Timothy O'Leary

Page 129 – *Possession* by Charlie Hughes

Page 136 – *Doing Time On A Pebble* by Paul Stansbury

Page 150 – *The Wheel Of Misfortune* by P.J. Sambeaux

Page 156 – *Let Zombies Live, As It Were* by Daniel LaPonsie

Page 166 – *Author Biographies*

Abstract Jam / Issue 2 / March 2016
ISSN 2059-8475 (print) / ISSN 2059-8483 (online)
Edited by Sam Leng / Website: *www.abstractjam.com*

Cover Art © Sophia D
http://bittersoda.deviantart.com

Cornucopia

By Terrance Gutberlet

It wasn't shocking that Uncle Michael wanted the refreshments at his wake to be served on his formaldehyde-preserved corpse. Most of the mourners merely dismissed the stunt with a sort of bemused head-shaking disbelief. Mitchell surveyed the cornucopia of refreshments: crackers, dips, rolls, pastries, ham and turkey rolled up and fastened with those toothpicks topped with red, yellow, and blue cellophane ribbons, the fruit tray, the cheese tray, and two other trays whose silver shafts, nestled between his arms and torso, seemed to rise out of his body. He caught himself smiling. A crockpot of steaming meatballs were wedged between Uncle Michael's thighs.

Uncle Michael might have howled when he came up with the joke, but he wasn't able to reap the harvest of his joke-sowing: the reaction of his audience.

Mitchell, meanwhile, had stopped smiling altogether. He saw that below the food was just a cold body. And below the body – Mitchell pushed a breath out of his nostrils at this – was a bed of grass. He saw two leaves sticking out of the ears and this stopped him from thanking his uncle aloud, deciding instead to give his thanks silently because, after all, Uncle Michael, the man who supported Mitchell and his Mom after his Dad died, was past the point of hearing.

Few of the mourners ate of the refreshments on and around the corpse. Mitchell figured that most of them found it tasteless, even for Uncle Michael, probably feeling that the joke was overwrought if not a little disturbing. At the same time – maybe contrary to Uncle Michael's wishes – it did little to diminish the gravity of the loss.

There was Caroline, his daughter, trying her best not to speak because her words trembled when she did. An elderly, bespectacled colleague from the hospital stared intently at the face, as if he feared it wouldn't keep in his memory. And a friend of Uncle Michael's, who wore a gray pony-tail, ruefully smiled as he lifted some grapes from a semi-circular tray surrounding his buddy's head like a halo.

Mitchell would have liked to hear their thoughts, but he didn't want to get caught up in some long conversation that would veer off – it was inevitable – to the point where he had to struggle to think of something more to say.

Because of that, Mitchell hadn't moved from the refreshments since running the gauntlet of introductions on his arrival, the kisses on the cheek, the handshakes and hugs and how-are-yous. It was a reliable strategy. Most people don't expect one to chat with a mouthful of food, so he kept scooping more spinach dip onto his plate. He watched a drop of it land on the edge of Uncle Michael's sleeve, a hair away from dripping onto what now seemed a rubbery yellow prosthesis of a hand. He stared at the drop of dip. It was large enough that others would notice. He wouldn't have hesitated to determine that it was the caterer's responsibility to clean it, but this wasn't a tablecloth. It was his Uncle Michael's nicest suit – a tuxedo at that.

He left the drop there anyway and his eyes caught the glare from the bald spot on the corpse's head. It appeared to have been waxed and buffed. The eyes were closed, but over them were his signature glasses. On Alexander's insistence, Mitchell thought. He was shaking his head. "Does the dead man really need the glasses," he mumbled.

Even more conspicuous, though, was the mouth, opened in mid-voracious laugh, bearing both teeth and uvula. A sickening feeling came to him when he guessed at what the undertakers had to do to affix it, imagining wires and stents bent and wedged into torn gums and jawbones manhandled by thick, rubber-gloved fingers.

Once the gentleman with the gray ponytail placed his grapes on his plate and ambled back to his circle of conversation, Uncle Ed and Aunt Penny took the man's place at the head of the casket. They had walked arm in arm to it, but Uncle Ed removed his arm to steal a tear. Uncle Michael was his brother. He made no eye contact with Mitchell, only acknowledging him with a nod of the head. It seemed he was in no mood to catch up, to make chit chat with relatives. Mitchell could relate, but he would have liked it, though, if Uncle Ed had said something to him. Instead, Uncle Ed talked to himself, whispering, "What in the hell?"

Mitchell kept staring at the face, at the mouth and the teeth, at the grin, made possible, he assumed, by some extra financial incentive offered by Uncle Michael to the operators of the Bakhtin and Becker Funeral Home. Uncle Ed was also looking at the corpse, breathing deeply, his head bowed. Then he shook his head and shuffled out of the room. Aunt Penny remained, grinning at the corpse.

"Your Uncle Michael's gonna laugh all the way to the grave. And then some. Won't he, Mitch?"

"Until the face starts decomposing," Mitchell replied while spearing some meatballs. He wondered if what he said was a little much, if he was telling her something she didn't want to hear. At least, he consoled himself, it was an honest, interesting comment. He was readying an apology if she should show any sign of disapproval. "These meatballs aren't bad," he continued. "Have you tried them?"

She didn't respond. Something else had caught her attention. She placed her wrinkled hands on the casket wall and peered into it more closely. She examined the arm. "You have some dip on your sleeve here, Michael," she said to the corpse. "Let me help you get this off your tux there." She took one of the napkins sticking out of the tuxedo jacket pocket as if they were pocket squares and scrubbed the sleeve.

"There you are, Michael." She scrubbed one last vigorous time and smoothed his sleeve. "You're welcome"

Mitchell put the meatball back on the plate. He stared at her. Speechless. He knew she didn't really expect a thank you, but still... That mound of bloodless veins and shriveled organs encased in yellowed flesh like a spoiled sausage from an Upton Sinclair nightmare will not thank you or tell you any more jokes or throw you any more witty rejoinders. He's dead. Is he not?

Aunt Penny put her hand on Mitchell's wrist and kissed him on the cheek. "It's good to see you, Mitch. I need to see where my husband went off to. Keep enjoying those meatballs. It's making your Uncle Michael very happy."

She smiled on the way out and rubbed her hand up and down the back of Cousin Jerry who had taken up a spot by the small cheese tray that must have been glued atop the corpse's shoes. Cousin Jerry had also been busy gorging himself, but for a different reason than Mitchell. He pointed at the cheese tray. "His toe cheese is delicious." He guffawed.

Mitchell smiled politely.

"How are the meatballs?" Jerry asked.

"They're good, but I think I've had more than I can eat. You want the rest?"

"Bit off more than you could chew, eh Mitch?"

With the refreshments no longer a place of refuge, he was left with only a few socially acceptable and self-permissible options. None ideal. Option # 1: Sit down and page through one of the photo albums scattered on the tables in the room. This problematic tactic, though, would likely draw another person of a curious bent. They would see Mitchell absorbed in the album and would assume he found something worth looking at, and since the only places to sit were on the couches, made to accommodate two to three people, someone would see the unoccupied cushion neighboring Mitchell as an invitation and with his luck it would be Aunt Eliza who was not easy to bear; Option # 2: Stand and look at the wall covered with awards and honors and photographs of Uncle Michael (in his pajamas, in costume, in his Dodge Viper, in the Hilton hotel he stayed in after winning a trip to Atlantic City on the *Price is Right*). But this presented the same problem as the photo albums in that, again, someone would see that Mitchell had found something worth looking at, notice the unoccupied standing space at his right or left, and take that as an invitation to come and look with Mitchell with the expectation that they would bond in a spirit of commentary; Option # 3: Install himself in a circle of conversation, suffer through the introductory chatter, though there was a chance that step could be skipped if the conversers were deep in discussion, and lay low, leaving the others to do the talking, himself adopting the role of interested observer who delighted in listening so much that it would be tacitly understood by the others that he didn't wish to spoil it with the type of responsive commentary that characterized active participation.

Mitchell opted for # 3, and found it in a group of people that included Caroline, Uncle Michael's son, Alexander, and Roderick, a rhinoplasty surgeon and friend of the family who was also one of Uncle Michael's closest friends. Caroline's eyes darted without moving her head. Alexander and Roderick were in the middle of a conversation.

"There he is," Alexander said. "Where's your plate, Mitch? Eat all you can. Dinner's on him tonight," he said, pointing at the coffin.

Mitchell laughed.

"Hopefully he doesn't croak when he sees the bill," Alexander said.

Alexander and Roderick started to laugh. Mitchell stopped.

"Well, how you doing, Mitch?" Roderick said with an extended hand.

Mitchell was still looking at Alexander, but after a delay he turned to Roderick and said he was fine.

"How's your mom?"

She was delirious, and would be in a home if not for her sister, but he said she was fine also. Roderick and Alexander kept him on the hook, prodded him for more information, so Mitchell told them of where he was living now, what he was doing for work, and all the other standard updates that he reluctantly, yet courteously, offered. When he was finished, Caroline, sniffling, bleary-eyed, possibly and probably medicated, gave Mitchell a weary smile as she started to walk away. She was about to pass him, so he took a small step and leaned forward, as if to hug her, but she continued walking to some other corner of the room, unaware of Mitchell's intention.

He regretted that he failed to say something to her, but Alexander was still there, and Mitchell wanted to ask him how he was doing. He took a breath as if he was about to speak, but the question he was going to ask, how are you, seemed silly. Mitchell didn't need to ask. Alexander's father was dead and he was acting as if he was still alive. That said it all. Mitchell took another breath and fell back on the tried and tired – yet ever-pertinent – subject of what was "new" with him. When Alexander finished telling him, Mitchell had no comment for him, no questions (he was sure he would think of some later), nothing at all by way of a volley to continue the conversation. There was a long, wordless moment, which led Alexander to turn his body away from Mitchell to look at the other goings-on in the room, leaving Mitchell to think that even a practiced conversationalist like his cousin didn't know what to do with Mitchell.

"Uh-oh," Alexander mumbled with an eye on the entrance to the room. "Look who's back." It was Uncle Ed, frowning and heading for Alexander.

"Alexander, what the hell is going on here?" Uncle Ed asked.

Alexander glanced from side-to-side. "There's a problem?" He knew there was.

"Yeah, there's a problem." Uncle Ed was nodding. "What the —" Uncle Ed checked himself, then continued. "What is that in the bathroom? It's sick."

Mitchell leaned forward a little, scrutinizing his uncle's face for his meaning.

Alexander hesitated, then nodded knowingly, as if he had prepared a response, a defense that he knew would be ineffectual. "Uncle Ed, it's what he wants." He started shaking his head. "I'm sorry."

"Don't give me that, Alex. If your father wanted strippers and circus freaks cavorting about, would you have made that happen, too?"

Laughter. Even from Alexander.

"Well, Uncle Ed, I don't think he would ask for that."

"I don't see why not. He *asked*," he said, emphasizing the past tense, "for all this other crap." He motioned toward the refreshments.

"Then I suppose I would have to respect his wish."

"Alex, come on. He was sick when he planned all of this."

"*This* is what he wants," Alexander said.

"Well, I'm not gonna use it." Uncle Ed opened his eyes wide and leaned his head forward. "It's disrespectful."

With a trace of — what was it, Mitchell wondered — melancholy or guilt or maybe just genuine penitence, Alexander responded: "I'm sorry you feel that way."

"So what am I supposed to do? Go outside? Didn't you consider — he consider, excuse me. Didn't *he* consider that some of us wouldn't be comfortable with this?"

Alexander remained silent.

What were they talking about? Mitchell looked to Roderick to see if he understood, but he looked as confused as him.

"Eddie, what are you talking about?" Roderick asked.

"You haven't been to that bathroom yet?"

Both Mitchell and Roderick responded with a shake of the head.

"He has a photograph of his face, with that shit-eating grin of his, literally," he said, taking care to control the volume of his complaint, "pasted inside every urinal and toilet in the goddamned bathroom." He faced Alexander again. "You couldn't have left *one* without it?"

Now this was a welcome development. An excuse to leave the viewing parlor.

What Mitchell saw in the bathroom was more or less what Uncle Ed had described. Photos of Uncle Michael – mouth wide open in the same fashion as the corpse – had indeed been taped or stuck to the inside walls of the urinals. Smaller photographs were placed underwater in the toilets. The photos had been laminated. A caption was written above each photograph in the white frame: "Fear not. I don't mind. You shouldn't mind going either."

It reminded Mitchell of his first car. A gift from Uncle Michael. It was used, yes, but it was free. When Uncle Michael drove to Mitchell's house to present the gift, he had left fake dog shit on the front seat.

This most recent scatological prank, because of the captions, seemed to carry a meaning beyond the obvious. "Fear not. I don't mind." He doesn't mind what? Going? Dying? And all the rest shouldn't either? Okay, Mitchell conceded. A worthy exhortation. Why fear the inevitable? Yet the "I don't mind" bit sounded like his uncle was trying to reassure *himself* that he wasn't afraid, for the very reason that he was, indeed, afraid. Like he was trying to beat death.

Mitchell wandered out of the bathroom, troubled by the scene. To think of how crushed his Uncle might have felt when he found out that the life he so thoroughly enjoyed had been given an expiration date – it was too heavy to carry back into that minefield of socialization in the viewing parlor. Mitchell stood in the lobby and looked at the black felt signboard and at the white letters spelling out *Michael Enoch Nicholson*. The 'h' in 'Enoch' was slightly askew. He stared at it until he lost focus, until the letters of the name floated off the black background, swirled counter clockwise, in a reverse gyre, into tighter and tighter circles until they disappeared, as if flushed away. He refocused and the letters reappeared on the black signboard, ordered on and reconciled to its furrowed field of rows and ridges. When he looked away, he saw Uncle Ed standing outside the glass doors, urinating on the building.

* * *

Back in the viewing room, after tiring of the lobby and its sobering color scheme, Mitchell overheard Aunt Penny saying that similar photographs were placed in the women's restroom. It was assumed that Caroline, as the only daughter of Uncle Michael, had the responsibility of placing the photographs there. She was wiping her eyes, sitting on one of the couches taking refuge in the arms of someone Mitchell didn't know. Some of the mourners had heads tilted down, lips parted slightly, restless eyes, expressions of condemnation. They appeared clannish, distant. They snuck glances of this woman who – it was evident to Mitchell – had felt as disturbed as they. Alexander, on the other hand, subject to the same semi-veiled derision, was standing upright as ever, unwavering in his belief in the virtue of executing his father's will in absolute fidelity.

"It wasn't her, was it?" Mitchell asked Alexander.

Alexander shook his head. Cousin Jerry was with him.

"You think there's a point to all of this?" Mitchell asked. "Other than the shock value."

Alexander smiled. "By asking that question it seems you might already know."

Mitchell returned the smile. "Well, yeah, but since you set everything up, I thought you might have a more definitive idea. He being your father."

"My idea." He nodded his head slightly. "I think it's similar to yours."

"Well? What do you think?" The coy act had begun to put Mitchell off.

"I saw you eating the refreshments earlier." Alexander turned to Jerry. "You, too, Jer." He then looked toward the cornucopia atop Uncle Michael, rising above the walls of the box. "There's plenty more. Pluck a grape or two or rake some more dip while I leave for a minute." He turned to walk away and Cousin Jerry, who didn't need to be told twice, embraced this charge and made for the refreshments. As he was leaving, Alexander addressed Mitchell. "Like I said, wait a minute. I'm going to have all of us gather around my father. It might help you figure out what he wants to say."

What *he wants* to say. He *wants.* Alexander with his present tense nonsense. As he walked out, Uncle Ed walked in. He was called by his younger sister, Eliza, the mother of Cousin Jerry. Mitchell overheard Aunt Eliza telling him to get his panties out of a bunch. Uncle Ed began to say something, but she cut him off.

"It's Michael's damn funeral, not yours, Eddie."

Uncle Ed nodded his head and walked away. He took a seat at the end of the room opposite the coffin.

Mitchell shook his head. "Heartless," he said under his breath. She had been giving Mitchell a hard time for years, too, ever since she found out that Uncle Michael was footing the bill for the tuition payments. It didn't help that Jerry was always struggling in school, struggling after school, struggling to find a decent job.

Uncle Ed was sitting. He was alone. He was no longer frowning. His shoulders were a little slumped. His eyes downcast. He wasn't angry any longer; he was dejected. A sixty something year old man scolded by his younger sister and desperately wanting, but helpless, to stop his older brother from making a spectacle of his death.

Mitchell took a step toward him, having the idea of sitting next to him to talk about the sham around them. But it was only one step he took. Would it embarrass Uncle Ed if Mitchell brought it up? Would he snap? What then? Mitchell would've talked to him about something else, anything else, if he could think of something, just so he could keep his uncle company. Where was Aunt Penny? Still giving him the same space as earlier when she remained to admire the corpse while her husband went off to feel like shit in solitude, in his damning solitude? Mitchell was going to walk over there, he decided, but, just as he was beginning to try to summon the resolve to do it, Alexander returned.

"Excuse me, everyone. Excuse me." He was holding a basket. So was

Roderick. "I'd like to have everyone gather over here by my father. In a circle. There are some chairs up front. Please." People hesitantly walked over to the coffin. "My father wants everyone to take one of these masks out of this basket."

Your father can't *want* anymore, Mitchell wanted to shout at Alexander as he put on a Ganesh mask.

"He wants," Alexander said, "you to put on the mask, and share a funny story or a humorous anecdote about him."

The mourners began pulling masks out of the baskets. Roderick passed them out to the ones less interested in participating. Uncle Ed, for one; Mitchell, for two.

"What in the hell," Uncle Ed said to Aunt Penny, "is this all about?"

The masks had proboscises. Long noses of men, fantastical creatures, demons, animals, masks in the Venetian style. Some laughed and shared their delight over the masks. The woman with the chicken nose, the man who picked the proboscis monkey, a bulbous-nosed Richard Nixon mask claimed it wasn't a crook. Aunt Penny took the Pinocchio mask. Mitchell was given a unicorn horn. He did not put it on.

One of the masks did not have a nose. Uncle Ed got it. Alexander gave him a skull mask. It was vintage Uncle Michael. Too perfect not to have planned. Irreverent to his own program of reverence.

"Okay, everyone," Alexander began to say. His voice was muffled. "You'll notice that the masks all have over-sized noses. Consider this a celebration of the body. Let's revel in our big, ugly noses. No need to fear or ignore these strange vessels we inhabit, no need to hide from the fact that our bodies will eventually pass away. What my father wants us to know is that, afterwards, we all remain in so many other, less obvious ways. So let's beat death together. Put on the masks. And don't be shy." He pointed at Mitchell.

Mitchell held the mask in his hand.

"You too, Mitch," Alexander said.

Others, too, were looking at Mitchell. He hesitated. *Beat death?* He wavered. *Celebration of the body?* He tightened his grip on the mask. *This is ridiculous.* He slowly lifted the mask just below his chin, thinking of how uncomfortable it made him to pretend he's something he's not, thinking of the costume parties where he showed up without wings or cape or zombie makeup, of the times he claimed to be dressed as orphan, delinquent, or in normal kid costume to get the candy on Halloween.

"Come on, Mitch," Aunt Penny urged. "For your Uncle Michael." She accidentally poked his cheek with her faux-wooden nose. She didn't notice.

Aunt Eliza, on his other side, also applied the pressure: "Remember all those cotton candies he got you at all the baseball games? You ate the hell out of those! The boardwalk, too. Christ, you lived in those damn bumper cars. And I don't even need to mention the college." But she did.

And of course Mitchell remembered. He turned red. Yes, Uncle Michael took him on those trips. Paid for everything. Not only food and lodging, but the price of admission, endless rides on the zipper, souvenir ball caps, many a chance to win a big, stuffed bear. And it wasn't only the small things Uncle Michael gave to him. Bigger things, too. Clothes, down payments, loans. Warmth, also. Amusement, compassion, generosity. Mitchell's own father had died before ever getting a chance to do the same, and Mitchell's mother never had a lucrative career. They always struggled with money. Mitchell did not need to be reminded, did not need to be told how indebted to his uncle he was. Nor did he need them guilt-tripping him into putting on that fucking mask. He looked around. Uncle Ed was adjusting his, visibly uncomfortable, but he was wearing it. Caroline wore one, too. And everyone else seemed to be at ease with it. Mitchell admired the mask – in his hand, on the heads of the others, the coming-together of it. But, they were prodding him, and so was the key to the car in his pocket.

While he had his hand in his pocket, digging the key in his thigh, Roderick took the pressure off of him and shared a memory. 1994. Monday Night Football. San Francisco 49ers vs. Kansas City Chiefs.

"Michael, forgive me," Roderick had said. "I'm confused. Are you a 49ers or Chiefs fan now?"

"Roddy boy, today, I'm neither. Just a Joe Montana fan."

"You made that?"

"It's easy. Cut two jerseys in half and sew them together. You don't have to be a plastic surgeon."

"Hardy har har," Roderick had said. "So who will you cheer for?"

"'9ers still. Ideally, San Fran will win the game despite Montana having the game of his life."

Mitchell remembered this. The two jerseys sewed together. A carnivalesque motley of red and white. Fondly lost in the memory, made unaware of himself by it, he glanced at Uncle Michael's laughing face (though it was not the face that was laughing but only the mouth), and, uncovering a mental image of the living mouth before the grim business of fixing it up, Mitchell put on the mask like everyone else.

Uncle Ed spoke next.

"Michael was my brother," he said. His voice was cracking. He paused to steady it. "So I know as well as anyone, if not better, that he was a clown, absolutely. But I don't think he would ever," he said, becoming stentorian, "want this grotesque farce if he was in his right mind."

Alexander took off his mask and opened his mouth to speak.

"I'm not blaming anyone here," Uncle Ed said.

Roderick put his hand on Alexander's shoulder. Others took off their masks. Mitchell, too.

Uncle Ed continued. "But these are the wishes of a dying man. 'Fear not.'" He sniggered. "He was afraid. That's all. He was trying to convince himself...that he would never be dead...or alone." Mitchell looked across the circle at the man in the pony tail. He had his eyebrows raised. Others locked their jaws, opened their eyes wide. Uncle Ed shrank back to compose himself. "I just want to ask you all to remember *him,* and not all of this."

The people were speechless. Aunt Penny rubbed Uncle Ed's back, but he gently stopped her. Mitchell had nodded his head when Uncle Ed mentioned the fear. But he was wrong about Uncle Michael being alone. All of the masks laughing, communing with each other was just what Uncle Michael wanted. Mitchell remembered that he had seen the man with the pony tail grin and make the sign of the cross as he took a roll from Uncle Michael's body. Mitchell knew that Uncle Michael must have been grinning, too, at the end, dying in his bedroom.

"Thanks, Uncle Ed," Alexander said with effortless sincerity. "I want to thank everyone for coming," he began. "My father's happy about it, and I hope," he said, looking at Uncle Ed, "that you take something from this rather atypical memorial service. The masks are gifts. Party favors. Wear them to some other party or on Halloween or as a joke. That's what they're for. Again, my father wants you to enjoy them. He likes his costumes, no? I know a lot of us here saw the full body drunken pigeon costume with the beak trapped in the plastic six-pack rings, right?" The memory brought some smiles. "And the Flag Day costume? Anyway, thanks for coming."

The mourners began hugging and kissing again, saying good bye. Uncle Ed left without a word. Mitchell still hadn't got the chance to commiserate with him, but that desire had passed. Instead, he watched Alexander; he watched Caroline. The former was talking and smiling; the latter standing near the corpse, no more or less morose than she had been all evening.

Perhaps Uncle Michael truly found consolation in thinking of death as something fertile and communal. It was clear Alexander was consoled to some degree. It was equally as clear that Uncle Ed wasn't. But to Caroline, it didn't seem to matter. Mitchell was in agreement with her, total agreement. If it worked for him, then it worked for him. It was a consolation after all, like the prize on a game show. He wasn't going to win the big prize, the Dodge Viper of eternal life. The best he could hope for was the consolation prize, those two free, ephemerally exquisite nights in the master suite of participating Hilton Hotels that only left him *feeling* like he'd died and gone to heaven. What she and Mitchell thought was of no importance to how her father, his uncle, got through it all. And while he was watching Caroline, a welling of compassion stirred him to walk over to her. He stood next to her. She was sniffling still. He put his hand on her shoulder and she embraced him.

Standing over the box, Mitchell looked at the coagulating meatball sauce, at an empty and smeared and becrumbed plate, at a corpse. There was a roll left. Mitchell took the bread off the body, broke it in two, and offered half to Caroline. She took it.

"Transubstantiation?" Mitchell asked.

And the two of them shook their heads and laughed, chewing the bread and looking inside the box together, seeing an inconsolable and undeniable end.

Funhouse

By Michael Tager

"When you wish upon a star," Joe sang. Phlegm rattled in his chest and he coughed, a deep wracking sound. He'd been talking to himself a lot: when he brushed his teeth, when he stared at his fleshy face in the mirror, when he stared out his kitchen window at his animal-kingdom lawn. His parents died long ago, his few friends drifted away after Kate left and his internet got shut off last week.

"Looks nice and open out there," he said as he lit a cigarette. He breathed dragon-plumes through his nose and looked at the lawn, cup of coffee in his hand. The house was a rat's nest that he hadn't cleaned in years; he was pretty sure there was something dead underneath the boxes in the basement. He wasn't going to find out. Instead, he looked for space to think, to make his peace. "Got too much on my mind." He took a sip of coffee.

The coffee tasted like dirt; when he looked down, he could see cigarette ash floating on the surface. Just next to the window was a sink, piled high with dirty dishes. When he threw the coffee in, it splashed back and drenched his threadbare blue robe, plastered it to his large gut. "Goddamn." With a snarl, he backhanded the pile of dishes. The resounding crash felt good for a moment, before his pounding heart caught up to him. He looked around for a place to sit. Every surface was covered with civil war memorabilia bought through QVC. He scratched his doughy, clean-shaven cheeks and squinted into the sledgehammer sunlight. His pale blue eyes underneath a heavy brow eventually adjusted.

Outside, just by the hydrangea bush that Kate planted the day before she left, Joe saw a half-hidden bench. It looked a good place to rest, to sit and think about everything on his mind since the diagnosis came back terminal. Once out the grimy glass sliding door, he slipped his feet into a pair of sandals that were covered in mold and moss from countless seasons outside, took a pack of cheap cigarettes from a robe pocket. He lit one and coughed after the first drag.

"Well, Joe, it's a jungle out here." He gathered breath. "Someone should clean it up."

The grass was thigh-high, the mulberry trees hadn't been harvested and the yard was covered in overripe, purple fruit. Underneath the berries were uncountable rat corpses and an ocean of cat feces. "What can you do, Joe?" he laughed.

Joe waded through the harsh grass to a forgotten pond, half-hidden by the hydrangea bush. The granite bench, he saw, was engraved with a "J & K", surrounded by a heart; Joe remembered watching Kate carve it. He frowned and pushed down the churning in his belly.

It was summer, and the bench was guarded by creeping ivy, weeds and prickly bushes, fed by the scum-filled pond next to it that smelled of rotted garbage. He just managed to fit his wide bottom on one corner of the bench and smoked another cigarette in peace. Sweat soaked his dirty undershirt, blended it with his flabby white torso. He rubbed his bald head, wiped away sweat, and stared at his reflection. It stared back.

"What ya think?" he asked the reflection. His reflection glittered, but stayed silent. It was as ugly as he was, had the same pockmarks and the same overbite. Kate had asked him to get some dental work done, if it bothered him so much. He'd brushed it off as her trying to change him. Now he wasn't so sure. Maybe she wanted the best for him, like she'd said.

Something about the pond and the sad, neglected bench, made Joe feel lighter. His doctor told him there'd be stages of grief, starting with denial and ending with acceptance. He wasn't sure; he hadn't been paying much attention. He wasn't sure he wanted to move through stages, but the longer he sat, the more thoughts (of Kate) seeped into his head: her dark hair and crooked smile, how she'd spent most of her time out in the yard while he watched TV. He pondered as he scratched his itchy legs.

"Ow," he cried and slapped his naked shin. A splatter of blood filled his hands. A mosquito twitched in his hand, blood oozed from its shattered body. "That'll teach him, huh Joe?" He rolled the corpse in his fingers, flicked it into the pond and watched it float. The pond drank the blood and something glinted from deep within. Joe leaned forward, tried to make it out before he felt something by his feet.

His shins crawled with bugs: greedy mosquitoes mostly, though a beetle lumbered over one of his toe-knuckles and zipped into the bush before inspection. "That was rude, wasn't it?" Joe hopped, savored the long moment before he crashed down to the earth. He hummed, did a jig and his thick lips trickled saliva when he felt a satisfying squish. "That'll learn you."

Trampled grass, dirt and insect pulp before him, an idea came to Joe's mind, slowly, like an unwelcome houseguest. He wasn't the industrious sort – his father and many employers could attest to that – but moments of focus did happen. When he looked down at his feet, at the ordered nature of the grass, he felt a Zen-buzz hum through his body. "What do you think, Joe?" he asked. "Think we should clean this up?" He got on his knees.

So close to the ground, breath came dear. There was no wind to cool him and sweat poured down his cheeks. But a few minutes of work went a long way. He plucked weeds, yanked ivy and gathered up severed rat tails, heads and appendages. When his heart started a staccato beat and breath came in wheezes, he groaned and sat on quivering haunches.

"Maybe I can make this an everyday kind of project, before I go," he said. "Not like I got much to do." Joe had been fired when he started calling in sick, back in January.

He stumbled his way back into the house and gathered up tools from places Kate had squirreled them. He found a trowel buried to the hilt in a dead ficus; a push-mower in the basement, under a tarp; dungarees Kate bought him, neatly folded, tags still attached.

The next morning, Joe found himself in his pristine dungarees. With a cigarette between his teeth, he focused on one corner of the yard, by the flowerbed, and remembered the mornings Kate jumped out of bed to work on the lawn. He hummed, bent to transport carcasses and crap into plastic bags, didn't bother with gloves. When done, he used a weed-whacker to trim the grass to something a mower could handle. Finished, he lit another smoke.

"I can handle this." His reflection didn't respond. He stifled a grin, coughed, waited for his heartbeat to return to normal. "Kate would have appreciated this." He smiled, stood, flicked his butt into the pond, and went back inside.

Every morning since was spent in the backyard, working. But when his heart raced and his vision blurred, he'd stop, light up and talk to his mirror image. Sometimes he was sure the reflection would respond.

"What could I have done?" he asked once. "I told Kate that I wasn't ready to get married. It was up to her after that." The reflection was silent. "I was just being honest."

Time went on and Joe slogged through less filth and debris. By the end of June, the grass was mowed and the yard became an arena to pace back and forth between flowers and pond. Between smokes, Joe orated, created happy endings where he got the girl and the job and the respect he deserved. When finished, he'd fling a still-lit smoke at the pool. Sometimes he'd touch his chest, take his pulse, measure breath. He was getting worse, he knew.

After the yard was mowed and all the cat shit gone, he cleaned the bench. Scrubbing the years of moss off the stone bench took effort and he had to pause frequently. When Kate had put the bench in, she'd asked him to help. He did the bare minimum, he remembered, and let her do all the heavy lifting. When he was done, he looked at the pond for answers. Instead, he just saw himself. He rubbed his jaw, sighed and went inside.

"I feel good, Mirror-Me," he said on the last day of July. "I mean, not good." He smiled and smoked. "But I feel better. I feel like, you know, maybe the end wouldn't be so bad." Joe took a long, hard drag. A fit of coughing overtook him and he bent over, hacked into the pool. Drops of phlegm formed ripples, flecks of blood sank into the water. Something swirled, glowed a deep purple, and he said, "I could be wrong, of course."

"That wouldn't surprise me," a voice said. "You being wrong." When Joe's eyes opened, he looked all around. The backyard looked quiet, orderly and empty.

"That's weird." He flicked his cigarette. "What do you think?" he asked his face as ripples spread and disturbed the muck. "Think it's just my imagination?" The scum floating on the pond coalesced. Joe peered closer and saw his own goateed face, scowling. His fingers found his face and traced his chin: quite hairless.

"I think you're a jackass," his reflection said.

A moment passed as Joe locked eyes with the not-quite-him in the pond. The wind stirred cigarette smoke into his eyes. He coughed and shut his eyes as tears trickled down his cheeks. "It must have been a dream. I must have fallen asleep," he said. When he opened his eyes, he saw his reflection scratch his chin.

Reflection-Joe laughed. It was devoid of humor and gave Joe chills. "Pinch yourself." When Joe yelped, the reflection laughed. "See?"

"So, I'm not dreaming."

"No," Reflection-Joe said. "Still smoking?"

"Y-yes, um, Reflection-Joe," Joe said.

The reflection grimaced. "Reflection-Joe? No. That ain't gonna work. Call me RJ, if you have to call me something."

"Ok, um, RJ." His fingers to his neck, Joe checked his pulse. It seemed normal. "I tried to quit smoking right before Kate left." He paused. "Things didn't go as planned."

"Kate left you, huh? That why you're fat?" The mirror image winked and grinned: gold teeth sparkled where Joe's own teeth were missing. Joe forced a laugh and focused on the rising warmth that rose from his considerable belly upwards and outwards. He started to feel an opportunity he hadn't known he was hoping for. He leaned closer and his reflection followed suit. There were more differences than just hair. RJ was leaner, missed the sizeable belly that Joe carried from too many T.V. dinners. There was an assortment of tattoos on his bare torso: a sickle on his right breast, a series of tears leaked from his heart. An ear was pierced and there was a long scar along his rib cage that looked, to Joe's untrained eye, like a knife wound. "You're what I see when I look into one of those funhouse mirrors. You know what I mean?"

"I guess so," Joe said.

"Well, funhouse aside, we're married, you know, over here. Me and Kate."

20

"Over where?" *Have I gone crazy?* He slapped his cheek; his flesh wobbled and stung. RJ chuckled. Laughter rose from the pool distorted, like dirty bubbles popping.

"Just accept it, Joe. Over here is where Kate's actually married to you. Over here is where you own your dad's company. Do you own your dad's company?" A quick head shake. "I didn't think so; you don't look like the CEO of Joe & sons. Over here is where you're busy every night and you have a hundred friends and you get your dick sucked regularly. Over here, Joe, is where you're not a loser."

RJ was dangerous, confident, so unlike Joe himself. "What do you think, Joe?" RJ cracked a knuckle and waited for an answer.

"About what?" Joe replied though a cotton-lined mouth. Through parched lips, he tried to whistle a tune. One from his childhood. Only a few fragments of notes came out, almost unrecognizable.

RJ pursed his lips and finished. *If I only had a brain.* "C'mon, Joe, I want you to switch with me. Bodies" The reflection laughed. "I'm done with this scene. I need a challenge. I can take that loser life of yours and turn it around." Joe was surprised at RJ's directness, but didn't doubt his words.

"But why would you want to leave?" he asked. "If you have it so good, I mean." His voice was high and quavered - it mocked him. His reflection shrugged, as if it didn't matter. *He's so … cool.* Even in his head, Joe sounded like a fan boy, like his backbone had abandoned him. Joe winced, waited.

"Life gets stale. If I can take your terrible life and make it awesome like me, I can do anything, huh?" He laughed and the water rippled.

Joe wanted to agree immediately. He stuttered out a few notes through bloated, slug-like lips as RJ waited.

"Well? What's the problem, Joe?"

Another cigarette, a scratch. "Let me think a moment," he said. RJ scowled, but nodded. Joe turned away from the mirror and sat. There was so much to think about, yet his mind churned through sludge. He brushed aside his dubious sanity - "Might as well assume I'm not crazy." - though there were other concerns. Was his mirror-image holding something back? He had to assume so, but so was he. And, speaking of his impending death, should he feel guilty about not disclosing it?

Was this a chance he should take? There had been some sense of settling his soul under a blanket and taking a nice long nap. Shouldn't he try to reach for that? You only get so many moments to transcend yourself. *When you wish upon a star.* He thought of Kate and her tight dress and sitting in the garden together.

He turned. "What do I have to do?" His mouth was a sour desert, all saliva fled. Blood flushed his cheeks strawberry. Joe pushed reservations to a tight compartment he'd built in his belly over the years: disappointment was an emotion he came to terms with long ago.

From somewhere by his feet, RJ hauled up a blue plastic bag, took out three items. "See these?" he spoke to Joe like he would to a child, over-pronounced every word to make sure of comprehension. "We're gonna swap." He explained the rules to Joe.

Before Joe went inside, he paused. "How do you know this will work?" RJ squinted his eyes and frowned.
"Does it matter one way or the other?" When Joe didn't respond, RJ snapped his fingers. "Go on. I'll wait." Joe was sure he smirked at him as he walked away.

The house was dark and smelled of dust. He ignored the mess and the mold and made his way straight to the cellar. A cloud kicked up and covered him. There were stacks of boxes, unlabeled, and he sighed, impatient to get back outside, to the warmth and light.

Hours later, he made his way through the lawn, back to the pool. It was dusk and he could barely see RJ in the pool by the hydrangeas. "I'm here. What now?" He was covered in so much dust and sweat that it mixed on his skin as mud.

Seeing the curled lips and mocking eyes of his doppelganger, he wondered, *Do I trust me?* He shoved his doubt aside, locked it in a little box in his heart. "To hell with it," he mumbled. RJ laughed and made little daggers with the first two fingers on his hand. He pointed at his own eyes, then Joe's. "I'm listening," Joe snapped. He flicked a cigarette at the pool. He laughed when the doppelganger flinched.

A spell of gasps and wheezes attacked him and Joe's knees buckled. He fell to the bench, still clutching the objects in his hand. The ground blurred and swayed as his breathing came in quick gasps. He struggled to regain control, took quick drags between barking laughs. He rubbed his chest, forced the muscles to breathe. Eventually, red-faced with a clown-grin, Joe stood and faced the pool of water. His reflection glared between scum and floating filters.

"What was that?" RJ asked, eyes narrowed, nostrils flared. Joe whistled and shook his head. *Hakuna Matata means don't worry.* The doppelganger spit. "You know what, don't tell me. Let's do this." RJ held up the objects in his hands. "We're going to trade, your stuff for mine, one at a time. Start with your childhood crap."

RJ held up a yellow matchbox car and Joe started. He had the same one in his hands, only blue. When he showed his reflection, he nodded. "Toss it in, Joe."

The blue matchbox car fell into the pool with a nominal splash and pulled some of the floating scum with it. As it went, Joe felt a tug in his heart and a sucking sensation in his head. Memories of playing with the blue car on the green carpeted floor of the family room vanished. Instead, he remembered a cracked, sun-beaten driveway and a yellow car. At the base of the driveway, the yellow car crashed into a heavy mud-crusted boot.

When he opened his eyes, he saw the yellow car emerge from the muck and fly into his hand. It was dented on top, plastic windows missing from where the boot had crushed it. Joe's initials were painted on the bottom in red. More memories crashed into Joe in waves. RJ's father was a yeller, his mother drank too much; both punished RJ for minor infractions. He grew into a wary child, angry.

Joe shook his head to reconcile his new memories and dropped the second relic without prompting. He'd been instructed to, "Get something from your greatest success (whatever that could possibly be)." There weren't many successes in Joe's life. Finally, after pawing through a stack of papers from his short-lived time working for his father, he saw it.

"Employee of the month, huh?" RJ asked as he stared at the soggy, yellowish paper he held with fingertips. He brushed off some of the green slime. "Fancy."

For Joe's part, he was holding a receipt from Caesar's, dated March of that year. There were a lot of zeros to the left of the decimal. Joe could remember a seven-day rush of events, fueled by alcohol, caffeine and a series of laughing women. "That Vegas trip just happened" he said. He ignored a heady sensation in his belly. The reflection winked. "What about Kate?"

"Don't ask dumb questions, Joe." The reflection held something small. "Last one."

The diamond ring in Joe's hand was small, the stone modest. The ring had lay in a cupboard, inside an ancient ceramic ashtray. He dropped it after only a moment.

The ring dropped to the bottom with no audible sound. From the pool, falling upwards, was a plain gold wedding band. Joe waited for things to change. He lowered his head and closed his eyes. "Well done, Joe," RJ said, a tone of glee in his voice that Joe ignored. "Now put it on." When he complied, his vision blurred and RJ's cackle stretched, flattened, as if he rushed through a tunnel: wind screamed and stretched, pounded his face.

He tried to scream but couldn't find air, lips or thoughts.

Abruptly, he could see. He was in an immaculate back yard, staring at a white house with a white door, a clear pool of water at his feet. "What's going on?" he mumbled. His tongue felt thick, unfamiliar. The pool before him smelled like nectar-coated gasoline. With his fingers pressed to his temple, Joe's choked down vomit.

His clean-shaven, fat reflection stared at him. There was a strange expression on his face. "Something you forget to tell me, Joe?" RJ asked. Before Joe responded, his reflection closed his eyes and fell forward. Just as his face filled the pool, the wind blew and shattered the surface. When the water regained tranquility, there was no RJ in sight.

Joe sauntered toward the white door. He noticed the shade was down. *Come and knock on my door.* He grasped the handle with a callused hand, smiled and turned. It didn't open.

He squinted, sidled over to the window and put his face to the glass. In the kitchen was Kate, hands on her hips. She was heavier than Joe, remembered, thick around the waist. Her face was tired, plain, her glossy, full dark hair back in a bun and streaked with grey. When he knocked, she turned, frowned, stalked to the window, grabbed the shade and yanked it down.

Joe walked back to the door, confused. A moment later it opened and a large envelope, followed by two small, shiny objects sailed out. The envelope flopped onto the ground at Joe's feet. The two rings hit Joe between the eyes. He could feel trickles of blood. Kate's engagement ring lay at his feet. He opened his mouth to speak and the door slammed closed.

The bench by the well-manicured hydrangea bush was comfortable as he opened the envelope. There were piles of documents. Some were glossy photos of Joe with a variety of women. The pictures were grainy, but it showed everything Joe needed to see. The rest of the papers were what looked like court documents. A cursory glance was all he needed; he read the words embezzlement and fraud over and over again. He tried to whistle through dry lips.

The reflection in the clear pond stared into Joe's eyes as he opened his mouth, desperate for someone to talk to.

The Jar Tree

By MK Sauer

My pa always said that there was two things t' keep an eye out fer: blood 'n' spirits. Now, I ain't talkin' 'bout them alcoholic spirits, neither, but what my pa'd call shades, what my ma'd call demons 'n' I reckon what I'd call ghosts. My pa knewed I had what he called th' see-through eyes when I was not more'n three or four – not old enough t' help on th' farm, no more'n a few odds'n'ends – when I come a'runnin' into th' house, breathless 'n' wild-eyed, cockeyfed like a 'coon what have its tail caught in a trap talkin' 'bout how I sawed ma in th' lake, braidin' her hair 'n' singin' some sorta haunted song when she had been dead since givin' birth t' me.

He didn' believe me none at first, neither, 'n' not 'til I described her down to th' birthmark what on her shoulder that he knewed I spoke th' truth of it. He took me aside 'n' th' weight of his calloused hand on my flowered dress shoulder was none too light 'n' felt like th' weight of th' entire house upon my snickerin' collar bone that I knewed that somethin' was comin'. Like a storm likely t' break th' windas or rip th' door clean off; my hair stood up like th' wind was already a'kickin' up 'n' blusterin' like a great big'un 'n' pa's hurricane eyes spiraled down into my own.

"Now that they know you," he said, "they'll find you even more. An' not all of 'em will be friendly like. Your ma's an exception 'cause she had them see-throughs too, but you, if'n you give 'em half a chance, they'll drag you down with 'em into whatever pit serves as a home t' 'em 'n' even these great big hands won't be able t' save you. They's hungry. Hungrier than anythin' you've ever known 'n' more 'n enough t' sink a little girl like'n you. Now let's drive t' town 'n' talk t' Grandma Sutter, alright?"

Gran Sutter was th' closest thing we all had t' a doctor 'n' I reckon th' closest t' a learned woman we e'er had in our small town. (An' I only knewed it was small 'cause'a what Gran Sutter had told me one day when I was brushin' my hand across her blue, danglin' bottles 'n' they's was clinkin' 'n' makin' blue music when she done showed me a map o' th' world 'n' then pointed us out on it 'n' we weren't bigger 'n' a pinprick on a finger, drawin' a tiny dart of wellin' up blood.) Most of th' people in our town thought she was some sorta witch but Pa knewed th' truth 'bout her: if'n you had a problem, she more'n likely had a solution that woulda never e'en crossed your mind.

I was in th' back of th' wagon what we always used t' bring in th' canned beans 'n' jerky t' trade with th' Watsons down th' way 'n' t' take back whatever'n we needed, 'n' I patted Hector on th' nose 'n' rubbed his neck like'n he liked 'n' he nickered. My pa's hand flashed through th' doorframe 'n' as I passed him by in th' threshold, he looked down at me, not sayin' nothin', 'n' just looked like it was th' last time he'd ever see me. An' maybe it was.

I put my hand up 'n' felt th' bottom of th' hangin' bottles 'n' looked up inter th' blue sky of her thatched roof with one eye 'n' saw a dark wood beam with th' other. Together they made a wavy melted mess of splinters 'n' water, like a flood of matches. Gran Sutter was sittin' 'n' lookin' at me too, but unlike my pa, she was lookin' like it was th' first time she seen me. She gave me a piece of straw t' chew on 'cause she knewed how much I liked things 'tween my teeth, like'n I just needed t' feel every bit of me, even th' 'tween parts 'n' maybe 'specially 'em. Her rheumy eyes found mine but they kept on movin', like'n she couldn't stop readin' lines o'er 'n' o'er e'en though she was just readin' me. Felt maybe she thought I was a book, but pa just told me that's how they was. Like'n how I could bend my elbow back so's that I was what he says was double-jointed, Gran Sutter was somehow jointed in her eyes all diff'rent.

She began t' talk 'n' I listened, I really tried, but there was a boy behind her what would not stop tryin' t' tug on her sleeve: "They see you, honey girl," – she called me honey, like th' honeysuckle what grewed outside my house 'n' bloomed at night, like some backwards kinda flowers that din't know th' sun from th' moon, like'n how I confused forks 'n' knives all together – "and that means that the more you see them, the more they will try to get in your bones. They want all of you: your warmth, your blood, your life." He was sittin' on her lap all dog-like now 'n' I giggled 'n' she musta seen 'cause she stopped talkin' 'n' then looked around her 'n' for a bit I thought maybe she knewed too.

Then that little boy did somethin' I ne'er though a little boy could e'er do: he rushed me, like a real nervous-like bull gets in th' field when he can smell th' sows in th' air, but can't get at 'em, pawin' th' ground 'til there are ruts so deep I almost tripped 'n' broke a'ankle, an' I saw all his parts from when he was an e'er littler boy 'n' he was jumpin' 'n' laughin' 'n' playin' with a little girl too, so's I knewed that Gran Sutter once had been like me but I just couldn't imagine how long it had taken for her t' get all wrinkled 'n' stooped like a broken fence bakin' in th' sun with worms runnin' through all th' cracks 'n' eatin' her up in th' insides.

"You had a brother," I remembered sayin' only later, rememberin' that I was me 'n' not him. It was like we were th' same person for a blink – 'n' not a Gran Sutter blink that lasts 'cause it takes so much effort for her t' open her eyes up 'gainst th' weight of all 'em years pressin' down on her eyelashes – but a blink like'n I do, quick 'n' fast like a rattler bite – 'n' I sorta shivered in th' blue light of th' bottles 'n' felt as th' feelin' returned t' my left side, pin pricks so'n I had t' look t' see if'n I was bleedin' little drops like red fire ants. "An' he died. An' now he's here 'n' he wants t' be with you but you don't know 'cause you can't."

"But you do," she said, noddin' her head like a bird drinks up all th' water in th' puddles left by a midnight rain, "and you can talk to him and you can watch him, but you can't let him do more than that. It's a river between you two and he's a candle on a paper boat and you're the current. You can move and twist him around, but if he tips over, sure he'll go out, but you'll never be the same. There will always be a part of him in you and you won't be the same river, now will you? I know it's a lot to understand, honey girl, but it's important you remember this. Can you do that?"

I reckon I nodded. I couldn't know that there would e'er be anythin' more'n th' Civil War soldiers who clambered around like bow-legged skeletons missin' parts, clawin' at my 'ttenion like horseflies bitin' 'n' yellin' their names, like'n I was s'pposed t' tell their children 'n' gran'children what 'xactly they did in order t' die or t' get their names in some foggy part of history that no'un 'members anymore 'xcept t' see how well th' land's healed in seventy years from th' ruts they scratched in it, just like those impatient bulls. I couldn't know that there would be anythin' else'n dead, stringy-haired girls what'n killed themselves by drowin' in th' river 'n' their moldy hands reachin' out t' tell me with their green, muddy eyes that they were right still 'n' th' ones who wronged 'em deserved a fate worse'n gurgly mouths 'n' sticky mem'ries. I couldn't even know that there'd be anythin' more'n th' relatives of my pa 'n' ma who'd look o'er me like I was some blossom of th' earth meant t' carry on their lives in th' way they saw fit. There was six ghosts tellin' me how t' live my life, but I always kept them floatin' along th' river like'n they was s'pppsed t' 'n' ne'er let 'em touch th' banks or th' bottoms, or e'en th' low-hangin' branches.

That was, 'til th' Stranger rode in.

It was his horse that first caught my 'ttention. I was hangin' th' sheets up on th' clothesline 'n' watchin' th' white square flappin' in th' wind. A bit of my hair got in my face 'n' I brushed it away with my hand 'n' saw a' approachin' shadow make its way towards me, each white square eatin' up a bit of himself 'til I could trace th' pattern 'n' th' first thing I noticed was that there was nothin' 'bout him. If'n I was a river, he was a frozen lake that was so filled t' th' brink of cold, cold water, e'en th' fish at th' very bottomest were flashed so solid they'd ne'er move 'gain. Most people'd have one, maybe two of th' spirits danglin' 'round 'em like hooks waitin' fer fish, maybe some live bait writhin' at th' ends so's t' draw in chompin' teeth, hittin' all th' 'tween places, but nothin' on him but his shadow, 'n' that wan't even all dirty-like.

"Ma'am," he said, tippin' his hat 'n' cloppin' past, lookin' at 'em sheets flappin' in th' wind. There was bottles danglin' off'n his horse, clinkin' in th' wind, what reminded me of Gran Sutter's blue bottles that was now all chipped 'n' broken. What with her dyin' within th' last winter on account of th' famine 'n' th' sick stock. I hadn't e'en been t' her funeral 'cause of th' graveyards 'n' all of th' spirits what hung 'round 'n' clung t' me like fast-growin' moss 'n' prickled, dried scorpion tails. But ne'er once did I see Gran Sutter 'n' without her there t' remind me of what I had promised, it almost seemed if'n I'd just been waitin' for someone like th' Stranger t' come along 'n' make me want t' forget.

Wan't th' last he came cloppin' in, neither. I seen him cloppin' all o'er our town, askin' questions here, makin' observations there, 'n e'ery once'n awhile he'd taste th' dirt 'n' taste th' wind, but ne'er th' water 'n' e'en though I found it strange, when he knocked on our door, Pa ne'er turned him away like'n e'eryone else, just opened th' threshold up 'n' he walked in 'n' scooped his beans up with a rusty spoon 'n' talked a little when Pa'd ask him a question, but ne'er once did he ask me nothin' nor do more'n nod or shake his head when I asked him one.

"Why'n you so quiet-like?" I asked 'n' how I asked it, I hoped he'd understand just what I meant.

He stopped chewin' his bacon 'n' stopped pushin' his food 'round on his plate, squealin' th' knife – or, rather, th' fork – 'gainst th' tin 'n' makin' my ears ring inside my head 'n' shrugged. Said he was just born that way, he reckon. Spoke like he was a gentleman, kinda like how Gran Sutter used t' talk, but even more gentle-like, like'n he was more used t' readin' than talkin' 'n' din't quite know how t' say th' words out loud like'n how he pronounced 'em in his own head. That many words, ringin' 'round inside his head, like baby chicks 'afore they hatched, I din't know if'n I could ever learn t' do some'hin like that.

"So, then," I said, tryin' my best t' speak like a lady 'n' gettin' more than a' eye from Pa whose mouth was busy workin' on a piece of chew but I could tell he was givin' me a minute 'til I figured out he was tuckerin' t' chew me, "why'n you have so many bottles a'danglin' from your horse?

An' that stopped him dead cold like th' frozen lake he was. He almost choked I hit him so hard with th' question I thought was just gonna get him talkin' 'stead of us watchin' his jaw workin'. But even after all that, Pa just pat him on th' back like he did me when I ate too fast 'n' spooned my dinner up in th' hopes of gettin' t' my 'broidery real quick – th' only thing 'sides plantin' that I looked forward fer –'n' went back t' chewin'.

"Our guest is tired, Jeze," Pa said 'n' my heart just fell right down through t' my feet 'n' started gushin' out black blood right then 'n' there. It hadn't been more'n three weeks since I talked t' someone wan't dead nor Pa 'n' already I was nothin' more'n th' little girl he

30

imagined me t' be, e'en though I'd flowered more'n six years ago. Gran Sutter had walked me though it when I was a-thinkin' I was dyin', that th' spirits had finally gotten themselves inter me like charred wicks 'n' ashen paper 'n' there it was, nothin' more'n my womanhood.

"But—" an' with th' look he gave me, I shut up right quick 'n' clamped a hand o'er my mouth, usin' th' other t' clear th' table 'n' start warshin' th' dishes. I din't hear one more word out of neither their mouths 'til Pa said it was time t' sleep. I climbed up t' th' open attic – we seemed t' live more'n a barn, what with th' rafters makin' a hayloft 'n' th' floor bein' little more'n dirt 'n' hay 'n' th' walls bein' nailed wood painted bright red t' keep th' spirits 'way from me when I slept so's they wouldn't get too bold 'n' try nothin' – 'n' blew out th' candle 'n' slept like th' dead what always tried t' overturn themselves.

Was a rough hand what shook me deep in th' midnight hour – a witchin' hour as some used t' call it –'n' another deep shush t' keep me silent as th' Stranger hung half his body off th' ladder o'er th' main livin' place 'n' th' other half watchin' me square in th' face not three inches from th' end of my breath. His eyes burned e'en though he din't hold no candle 'n' th' moon wan't even out other'n God's thumbnail, like'n Pa liked t' say. Good for God t' keep us in his hand, he'd say, but bad for th' man what wants t' see more'n he should in th' witches' time.

I went t' talk but he just put a finger o'er my lips 'n' climbed up inter th' attic 'n' sat down next t' me in th' dark. I sure was glad that he prob'ly couldn't see more'n me, 'cause I was in nothin' but my gown what belonged t' my ma when she was still alive 'n' as sheer as it was, it weren't no proper thing for a stranger t' be seein' me in. I wondered if'n I should call for Pa when th' Stranger looked at me with those burnin' eyes 'n' asked how long I had been able t' see th' spirits 'n' if'n I could do a favor fer him. Said he knew when I asked him 'bout th' bottles hangin' off of his horse, Dusk, as he called her, what with th' dusky pallor 'round her hooves 'n' nose.

"I used to see them all the time," he confessed t' me, inchin' closer so's we could talk without Pa overhearin', "but lately I haven't been able to. I haven't quite figured it out, yet, but I was hoping to run across someone like you. I lost someone very close to me and I want to know if she's around and if she has anything to tell me."

"Oh," I said, tryin' not t' be disappointed, 'cause after all, he was a stranger 'n' it weren't like he owed me nothin', but it was disheartenin' somethin' awful t' hear him say her when I wanted him t' see me, e'en in my gown. Maybe e'en 'specially. "I first noticed you 'cause of th' deadness 'round you. I mean," I said, closin' my eyes, tryin' not t' let him know how much dis'pointment was a-poolin' up inside me th' more words came poppin' out of my mouth like some flash flood without no warnin', "a deadness of spirits. Which, now I say it, don't make sense, but t' me it does. There's nothin' 'n' I'm sorry if'n that's not what you want t' hear, but that's just th' way it is."

"Jezebel," he said, real soft like, like'n no one's e'er said my name 'afore. He put a hand t' my cheek 'n' it were th' first time someone touched me who wan't related t' me or Gran Sutter. All th' townsfolk been too afraid since they's all found out that I had 'em see-through eyes. His hands were softer'n Pa's 'n' since I never knewed what my mother's hands felt like, I imagined it weren't nothin' like hers neither. An' then he kissed me 'n' as much as I liked his hand on my cheek, I liked that e'en more.

"But, Pa might—" I responded 'n' he cut me off with another kiss as he began t' lift my gown up o'er my head 'til I was lyin' in th' dark, shiverin' 'xcept fer his warm body 'gainst mine stark naked, wearin' nothin' but my nervousness wrapped 'round me like a barrel. I never once thought while he was explorin' me in th' gloom that it weren't right nor that this Stranger was takin' advantage of me, just that I was lonely speakin' only t' th' dead 'n' here was someone who had been like me but gotten o'er it, had found a way not t' be a stream what trickled through life drop by drop, always waitin' for some pinprick or'n 'nother capsize or th' weight of th' sudden stoppin' of weightlessness t' bury me in some coffin, still alive but not breathin', not doin' nothin' but lyin', waitin' for th' day when I'd be unburied.

An' here's what this Stranger was doin': diggin' me up, all finger-like 'til he was inside me 'n' we was movin' together, seeds bloomin' deep within me, crawlin' through me in nerve-pinchin' ecstasy – a word just come t' me at that moment what I ne'er knew 'afore – 'til I moaned so

32

loud I thought Pa would hear 'n' thought he'd be redder'n any fire ant if'n he caught us up there.

We were both sticky with more'n sweat when I heard 'em, whisperin' in their jars like wind walkin' through tree leaves, decidin' who it wanted t' dance with 'n' then choosin' no one in th' end t' e'eryonoe's disappointment. I froze, all of th' little hairs on my arms standin' shock up with their faces wavin' in th' shiverin' chill 'n when th' Stranger reached for me, cuppin' one of my round breasts in his hand 'n' kissin' th' freckles on my back what always made th' shape of a bird as'n my Pa 'n' Gran Sutter said. They were comin' from th' outside right where'n we left th' horses t' sleep in what we called th' stables, which weren't more'n a roof 'n' four pikes in th' ground 'n' stalls made out of hay 'n' such.

"They's whisperin' after midnight," I said to th' Stranger. "I ne'er heard a spirit do that 'afore. It's always 'tween th' dawn 'n' midnight 'n' ne'er after. They don't like th' 'tween places much, not like me. No. It scares 'em more'n whatever waits for folks after they die. Which, I s'ppose, is why they're still here."

"What are they saying?" he asked, workin' his kissin' up t' my neck 'til he found th' pulse there 'n' stopped, just feelin' my life flowin' up t' my head, I s'ppose.

"That's just it," I replied. "There's just so many of 'em, I can't make out a single voice what could tell me what he wants. Can't see 'em, neither. They're too far away. Don't know what t' do. Never happened 'afore like this. D' you s'ppose it's 'cause of what we did?" I couldn't even tell myself if'n I wanted him t' agree or not, so's I just sat 'n' thought 'n' kept tryin' t' make out th' voices. They sounded angry, like a hive of bees buzzin' 'cause they know their nest's gonna fall 'cause they built it in th' wrong spot. It grew 'n' grew 'til he coasted his fingers 'tween my legs 'n' it was so silent that I could only hear myself breathin' as somethin' began t' dam up inside me.

When th' daylight hit th' side of th' house 'n' I wan't up yet, I told my Pa – worse, shameful moment of my life, but'n I had t' do it – that I weren't feelin' well an' if'n I could just lay in bed, I might get better. I din't wanna be gettin' anyone else sick 'n' I could tell from th' way th'

Stranger asked if'n he could help with th' chores that Pa knewed somethin' wan't right, but din't want t' be rude t' th' only guest in years. Under th' covers of my bed, I cried, but they were th' best tears of my life. Each trail down my cheek tasted salty, like blackened guilt, but after they was gone, I felt only th' happiness what I found th' night 'afore. All th' sweeter 'cause of th' salty ones testin' my tongue 'n' makin' it answer all false.

In order t' help 'round th' house I cleaned up a bit, my hands movin' of their own accord as my mind was elsewhere 'n' I almost broke th' only glass cup we had what we got from ma's ma who had once loved a glass blower; my own grandma stood in th' kitchen, passin' one hand through th' delicate veiny glass what looked like solid water floatin' there 'n' she told me with those blue, blue lips of hers treadin' th' river, gulpin' in my warmth like it were air. Grandma liked th' kitchen 'n' I reckoned some part of her was still dancin' in that vessel 'n' she had told me th' same story over 'n' over so much that I din't realize she looked diff'rnt, wavy 'n' smoky like heatwaves on th' backs of gallopin' horses 'til she put one watery hand on mine 'n' blew. All th' little hairs on my wrist rose 'n' when I locked eyes with her it felt like I was a keyhole tryin' t' fit th' wrong set of keys.

"Th' Stranger," she breathed 'n' it smelt like th' grave, a smell that done ne'er leave my nostrils no more, "you keep him in your sights, Jeze, darlin'. There somethin' t'aint right 'bout him. You see him through glass, now, 'n' you'll know.

It were th' first time what a spirit talked t' me 'bout somethin' involvin' me 'n' not just some dead part of themselves wishin' t' get a message 'cross or through or o'er or under. Spirits was all 'bout curves 'n' circles; ne'er did they e'er use a straight line. Time din't work for 'em like it did for me. I musta stayed shock still in th' kitchen for longer'n I knewed 'cause in waltzed my Pa 'n' th' Stranger 'n' th' two din't say nothin' as I gripped that glass 'til Pa had t' cup it in his hand 'n' put th' other on my raised hair wrist.

"Jezebel?" He only e'er said my full name when I was in th' direst trouble. "Honey?"

"'Twere Gran," I whispered. "Not Sutter, but our Gran, ma's ma. It just startled me, tha's all." I hated lyin' t' him a second time all in one day 'n' I prayed t' God that he weren't gonna punish me for it, but it'd be better if'n he din't know th' entirety of what I went through. It would break his already glassy heart. I din't look at th' Stranger, not til I stopped shakin', 'n' only then, it were t' hold up th' glass t' th' light, like'n I was checkin' it for water spots 'n' when I done brought it down t' put back onto th' dusty shelve, only then did I lookit him 'n' see that his shadow weren't quite in line with th' rest of him.

It — no, they — writhed like snakes or maggots wrigglin' in a decayed mass of afterbirth, like'n when I found a whole mess of bunnies what been half-deformed 'n' stillborn 'n' eaten by their mother 'cause she just din't want 'em, or couldn't have 'em, or what — I couldn't talk t' th' dead animals 'n' that was 'cause they don't have souls like what we do — but she musta died sometime too 'n' so there were so many bugs skitterin' 'n' scatterin' that it took me a full two minutes 'afore I realized just what it was I was lookin' at. His shadow were th' angry buzzin' bees I heard th' night before, twistin' 'round him like some sort of gauzy halo 'n' it weren't 'til I done took a step backwards, bumpin' inter th' counter 'n' smashin' my hip 'stead of th' glass.

"Okay, honey. How 'bout you go into bed early tonight. All right?" Pa said, his voice hollow, like thunkin' inter a' empty chest buried what under th' ground with th' head of a shovel.

That night I fixed supper for th' three of us 'n' Pa was more quiet than he was 'afore 'n' th' Stranger seemed t' have taken all of his words 'n' mangled 'em up in his mouth 'cause Pa was concentratin' in puttin' all of his words inter his eyes t' shoot at th' Stranger 'n' t' me he was just pale, like'n my faked sickness was catchin' 'n' it hit him harder'n me. I wanted t' say somethin', t' let him know what I knewed, but his eye couldn't see-through th' glass 'n' I din't know how he'd act if'n he figured it out. For once, th' river quieted, but it seemed like'n it was washin' Pa away 'n' my fingers weren't quite long 'nough, or maybe I just weren't reachin' too hard.

That night th' Stranger came up t' my hayloft 'gain 'n' this time we opened up th' roof t' let th' air 'n' stars in 'n' I watched 'em watchin' us 'n' fer th' first time I breathed 'n' it weren't dirt that came down my throat 'n' it weren't water, just air. An' I knewed it were 'cause of him 'n' those shadow wings of his.

A buzzin' woke me, close t' my ears like someone held a flame cracklin' real close t' my face but without th' feelin' of heat. It were th' spirits 'gain, 'n' when I reached o'er t' wake up th' Stranger, I found nothin' but that air that so fascinated me 'afore, but was no more'n chillin' 'n' empty 'n' space, but without any stars, just th' spaces 'tween. I crawled down th' ladder, wrappin' my gown 'n' th' sheet 'round me, not so brave without him there 'n' snuck out good without e'en makin' th' door creak.

Th' grass was cool 'neath my feet 'n' wet with dew, but not cold. Th' blades hit th' bottoms of my feet 'n' fer a blink I din't know if'n th' wetness down there was my blood or just th' collected imaginin's of all of th' grassy ideas – fer if animals can think but don't have souls, what 'bout th' e'erythin' else'n th' world? Grass may think just as much as I do 'n' who am I t' say it don't? – 'n' I cried out softly for th' Stranger, not knowin' what t' call him, 'cause I ne'er e'er knewed his name.

'Gainst my cheek shifted a slight breeze 'n' I had t' wipe away th' tracks of tears 'afore I noticed that it weren't no tears, but a slight speckle of rain. I ran under th' nearby copse of trees that bordered our land with th' neighbors 'n' looked up t' th' sky t' see a trail o' fireflies flittin' 'bout, avoidin' raindrops as much as me. I imagined I could a'hear 'em firin' up their lights 'n' blowin' in them coals t' wake up th' night. It weren't rainin' water no more, but ashy flakes 'afore I realized that they weren't no fireflies, but man-made lights twinklin' with 'n' movin' 'cause of th' wind.

I followed, like some mezm'rized moth, drawn by th' song of th' faked fireflies 'n' found a barky feelin' juttin' up 'gainst my fingertips as I looked up t' see hundreds of th' tiny glass jars from th' back of th' Stranger's horse grinnin' up in th' branches, tied off by stringy 'n' frayed rope, blackened with pitch 'n' smellin like burnin' hair. Seemed as if'n there were a small jar for each branch on th' tree, sad necklaces for th' many-necked beast with broken bones 'n' twisted head, eatin' 'n' chewin' each other 'n' in each jar sparked a tiny, little flame. 'Round th' flame was some angry buzzin' or what, liquefyin' 'n' coagulatin' inter some type of milky white swirls. Th' smoke from th' flames, which changed color dependin' on where you put your head, hit th' cork up top, curled 'neath itself 'n' then, gettin' tighter 'n' tighter 'til its dam burst 'n' then, white tears a-runnin' down th' glass, stainin' it 'n' collectin'.

They were all over th' place, so much so that I din't know how they e'en got t' th' top of th' tree 'til I saw th' Stranger, runnin' his hand 'neath th' bottoms like what I used t' do at Gran Sutter's place, only all th' blueness turned t' white 'n' there weren't no dead, no spirits, just th' empty sky, like e'ery branch of th' tree blocked out th' stars 'n' e'en th' thumbnail moon, leavin' no God, no eyes from above, but just th' angel with th' movin' cloudy wings. My heart beat loudly in my throat, so much so that I din't know how th' Stranger din't hear 'n' come runnin' or at least yellin' or a-sternin' like some great big ship what I heard tell 'bout, but ne'er actually seen. Like pinpricks on fingers 'n' maps.

He plucked one, like pluckin' an apple or a forbidden ev'nin' fruit, pungent 'n' flowerin' inside 'n' swirled it 'round a bit in his palm, warmin' it up with th' veins in his hand 'n' blowin' on it, just like my ma's ma described her love blowin' on th' glass what t' make it bigger 'n' bigger without breakin' th' flow 'n' breakin' th' skin. Pulled out th' cork with his teeth, he did, like I seen some of th' drink gnashers a-guzzlin' their spirits − th' alcoholic kind, like what I once thought th' dead were too, 'cause of th' similar name, you see − 'n' 'afore I could stop or call or nothin', he done what I seen them gnashers doin', 'n' he drank that spirit down til e'en th' candle went out in th' bottom of th' milky white glass. Maybe my eyes dropped out of my face then 'n' there, I din't know, but I knewed it froze me like clearin' 'way th' cobwebs of dead 'n' their fingerprints all over my own glass body.

He was a-drinkin' ghosts from th' tree full of hangin' jars, lightin' th' sky like man-made − angel-made − stars, pinpricks of light, not blood. I could only reckon on how they tasted 'cause I only knew what their words 'n' occasion'lly their paper hands tasted like in my own throat 'cause they could reach through. My tongue dried out at th' thought, like coatin' my entire mouth with th' burnin' whiskey what Pa done bring home sometimes t' forget. I could never forget what I ne'er knowed.

It were then that he heard me, gruntin' 'n' chippin' 'way at th' bark so's t' mark th' tree like'n my Pa showed me once so I wouldn't ne'er get lost in th' forest like I had when I was only three, which is when my Ma's spirit found me 'n' told me which way t' go back. I done did it out of nervousness more'n anythin' else, but th' Stranger sure heard me 'n' when he saw my hand just hangin' underneath th' tree, strung up by th' wrist like one of his jars, he scowled deeper'n anyone else I e'er seen.

"These are not for you," he said. "I don't know what'll happen if you were to ever touch one."

"Why'n do you have these folks' spirits? What'd they ever do t' you?" It weren't no accusation, but I din't quite know how God meant t' punish th' spirits when alls they ever did was be a mite annoyin', 'n' sometimes even a mite scary, but never done no harm, nothin' like I seen other people do t' other good folks. A ghost can't do nothin' t' you but watch 'n' hunger a bit 'bout you, but a man can run hisself right through you, choppin' 'n' hackin' 'til there's naught left but a bit of you that don't quite seem like how you was 'afore.

"These aren't like the ghosts you see, Jezebel," he said 'n' there it was 'gain, him sayin' my name like it were th' most beautiful thing t' say, but e'en then, a part of his tongue caught 'gainst th' top of his mouth, like'n he was 'bout t' try 'n' push it through all of his mem'ries 'n' get t' th' truth of it all, but was still tryin' t' figure out how t' tell a simpleton like me. Words were thick, like th' mud that sometimes collects under Pa's boots 'n' when we fish it out, we find still alive things, clingin' t' th' boot all crushed like 'n' strugglin' what t' walk with no legs. There was a wrigglin' in his words an' I remem'bred Gran 'n' th' things she a-told me. "They've done wrong and I've been tasked t' make them leave this place. You see, they were what killed the woman I loved. I hope that by capturing them and drinking them, I can make them tell me where she is."

I slowly walked toward him, thinkin' that he wouldn't think nothin' of it if'n I din't give him cause 'n' oh so slowly I moved myself under th' twinklin' of th' jars so'n that th' wavy 'n' circled bottom of one of 'em stood 'tween th' Stranger 'n' me so's I could get a look at him 'gain, 'n' see them wings 'n' see his words 'n' tell th' truth of 'em, like measurin' a worm 'gaint th' length of my pinky finger. Gran Sutter was th' one what told me that truth was th' longest thing in th' world 'n' anyone who weren't straight would be just as short 'n' curvy as them shades. Somethin' t' hide 'neath their freckled, see-through selves.

Through my left eye, what was lookin' at him all normal-like, I saw Th' Stranger just like'n I always do, but through my left, peerin' through th' bottom of th' glass just like'n I been told, there was his shadows 'gain, all shufflin' 'n' settlin' like what a bird does with its wings before it gets t' a-glidin' through th' sultry air. 'N' as I was peerin' through th' bottom of th' glass, I noticed that th' milky whiteness inside was growin' a face 'n' a nose 'n' was peerin' out at me like'n it knewed me 'n' was scrunchin' up his face t' press 'gainst th' glass 'n' make his breath known.

"Jeze!" it called, its ghostly little face all swimmin' through th' jar 'n' lickin' at th' side, tryin' t' get t' me. Now, I don't know what kinda shade e'er wanted t' talk t' me, usin' my name like they had some kinda thought other than th' one what 'em always had, but somethin' 'bout that voice recognized in me some kinda longin' 'n' I knew that it weren't no bad spirit 'cause it had been hangin' 'round Gran Sutter's place for longer'n I was born 'n' it weren't no cause of no woman's death, neither. It were Gran Sutter's long dead brother, shinin' out from th' middle of a glass jar.

I grabbed a'hold of th' jar, much t' th' horror of th' Stranger 'n' went t' threw it down t' th' ground, 'cause that's what I thought would be best, 'n' when my hand done reached for th' jar, it sorta collapsed in my hands, like it were made out of brittle glass what crumbles at e'en a thought. Th' ghost inside, Gran Sutter's lost brother, went a'screamin' toward th' Stranger, his mouth more wide open than th' groupers what dangle 'em mouths out for flies 'n' when he hit th' Stranger, it were like he got shot with a bullet that moved so slow, I could see th' puncture 'n' th' exit wound sprayin' out, like'n he was a leaky garden hose. But I knewed it weren't no water, but somethin' else, somethin' that was upsettin' all th' jars and they got t' twinklin' and swingin' in th' breezeless night 'n' one by one they started a-droppin' onto th' floor, breakin' their brittle selves until there weren't no whole jars left 'n' all the ghosts were attackin' th' Stranger, goin' inter his body 'n' leavin' their residues all o'er his insides, causin' 'em t' be on th' outsides until he weren't nothin' left but a shell of a man 'n' a woman ghost clingin' t' th' side of his soul, tippin' him this way 'n' that, like a ship gettin' swallowed by th' dark, demandin' sea.

I knewed then that he had been like me, but that hungry ghost – probably th' very self-same one he had been lookin' for this entire time, had somehow gotten inside him, tipped his soul-craft o'er 'n' began t' tunnel through him like a miner searchin' for his golden fate in th' dark bowels of some hellish mountain. Th' she-ghost shriveled 'n' then there weren't no more of him than just a tiny bit of milky-white glass, swayed by th' grass 'n' soundin' off th' last bit of him t' th' remains of his jar tree. I picked it up, bein' careful not t' cut my fingertips on th' ghastly edges 'n' waited for th' remainin' spirits t' settle back inter th' sweet earth.

Humpington Plantation: A Satire

By Mike Crumplar

It was a beautiful day on the plantation and I was swagging in my new designer petticoat, early adorned as per usual and carefully too. It was important, so delicate and promising that I felt there to be a sort of moral imperative, an imperative to the eros of fashion, an eros that the later heat would do nothing to sour. I observed Ellen as she exited the main house after an early breakfast while the dew was still wet on the grasses and drooled at the wetness of her feet from afar. I watched from the windows of the guest house graciously and indefinitely granted to me by Master Humpington, the master and overseer of the expansive Humpington Plantation. Ah, Ellen, the imperial pearl of Humpington Plantation, a world of meaning flows from the river of her pussy. All else is the mere décor—her bodacious blonde locks that dangled daintily on her pure white dress, her exquisite curves that gracefully yet firmly declared her womanliness. They are the frame of the sex, which takes the form of water and is boundless, oceanic. She filled the whole plantation with it, her silence led the work songs of the slaves, her long walks through the meadows beyond the tobacco fields endowed the plants with an aroma distinct to the crop, as she dipped her toes into the canal the whole landscape became pregnant with her essence so that only I could see it for what it truly was.

I returned to the guest house, for later I had business to conduct with Master Humpington. He was highly interested in my work, wanting to make it into a grand performance, and through it I was determined to assert my power and worthiness as a lover and possessor of his daughter. Such a work would be easy to write under the intoxicating influence of Ellen and her pastoral world—the overwhelming gaiety of Humpington Plantation. And for Master Humpington, it would be a ringing endorsement of his way of life, as a man whose industry converts untamed land into products and currency thereby humanizing them, turning raw matter into man matter, black beasts into workhorses, organizing and civilizing, and, in short—realizing. I am a man who admires industry and its products, and I believe that it is facilitated by great men of history, civilized men like Master Humpington. I knew I could win his favor through precisely this productive spirit—the industrious transformation of raw materiality into the erotic. Indeed, that is my specialty.

Soon I found myself by the canal once more, in the ecstasy of Ellen's trace that blessed my violin and spirit with a special guidance of purity and joy. I wrote a song of angelic whiteness—which sadly here I cannot even begin to describe—and with my tool, I lured her out of the lily pads and willows by the water, summoning and seducing her into the harmonies of the land itself. Such inspiration made it clear to me that there was a certain destiny I had to uphold, she was the water upon which the great ship of culture sailed, and I its captain, or perhaps the engineer of the ship, or perhaps the wealthy entrepreneur who financed its expedition. Her supreme wetness lubricated my inspiration and melody flowed ceaselessly by the canal, it would be her overture, through which she or her representation would emerge onto the stage and declare herself, sex personified and liberated, enabled. I thought of her song as the moment of realization, by which the world would finally know its own meaning—eras of history and evolution in the means of production adds up to the ultimate instance of erotic unfolding.

Ah yes—this would be my opus. To give voice to the ever silent Ellen, who had managed to elude me, despite my persistent voyeurism, my dream. Each smile and nod unreturned, but that is nothing, for I must only convince her Master for her ownership. I imagined walking through the tobacco fields holding her hand, leading her through the rows as the sun sets and the slaves have since left to their quarters, lust in mind while taking her to the waters for her to become herself. As she steps into the water her form fits to her body, nipples asserting themselves from inside her white dress in the cold, I grab her ass and she turns to me, smiling straight into my eyes but still silent. I could never imagine her voice. But such is life; the artist must erect the voice and words of woman when writing an operetta as they remain ever distant, absent. I would often invent words for her, words that fit the form of her grace and purity, I constructed a whole language of her thoughts, the language of restrained-yet-emerging vaginity. My imagination would drift on further down the river, ever further, into realms of pure fancy in the distant future, of pure boastfulness that could not be transcribed. I imagined ruling Humpington Plantation myself, wed to Ellen long after I had crystallized the legacy of her father and creator. It would be a life of pure joy and ecstasy, as I would be me in my fullness realized alongside Ellen in hers. Those thoughts governed my dreams in the night.

The next day was hot and humid, characteristic of the late Virginia summer. Early on, just as the sun was rising, I caught a glimpse of Ellen walking out from the Humpington mansion through the tobacco fields in her delicately flowing white dress. I was captivated and entranced like never before. I decided to follow her, in the hope of hearing her voice, which I suddenly felt could finally give me the last rush of inspiration to finish my work. So as to not alarm her, I trailed her from a distance, closely observing each of her graceful steps. As I followed her, I was quivering with anticipation, I felt that the moment my love would be realized—and raised to a higher power—was just instants away.

She reached the end of the tobacco field and was soon in the woods that stood beyond, where I could no longer track her so easily. The summer underbrush was dense and no path was clear. For several minutes I felt the sort of emptiness that an explorer on the open seas experiences, not knowing whether he will survive long enough to reach land or die in the middle of salty wetness. But I had the ruthless determination of Aguirre. Trapped in the brush, I felt a sudden, sharp pain. I pushed on, knowing that Ellen was somewhere near, tearing my petticoat on the thorns. Of course, that is no matter, as once I become rich from my operetta I will buy another of superior make. So I pushed on deeper in the woods, growing ever more excited with each passing moment. I finally reached the edge of a clearing—and there was Ellen with one of the negro slaves! In the center of this clearing, two shapes, dark and light entirely revealed, I gazed as Ellen's open mouth and tongue plunged into the ass of this negro, who I had noticed before as one of the strongest and most able of Humpington's slaves. Only the negro spoke: "Ya ho stick yr tongue in my ass" he demanded, and she was occupied with that exactly. "Cradle my balls," he added, and she continued. I watched in horror for several minutes—how could my future wife do this to me? And with one of the negroes, no less! My blood boiled and I stormed off, unwilling to confront this treachery. I ran through the brush and the tobacco field feeling a rage I had never experienced. The image of my Ellen—tongue deep in the asshole of Humpington Plantation's "Great Negro," her mouth and face caked in shit—rang through my head endlessly. I ran past the guest house to the canal, which was today a muddy, jizzy, silty brown. My mind and heart were racing, and I thought of the Nile, the sustenance of Ancient Egypt in its ebbing and flowing, covering the land with a layer of shit that brings about new life and epic monuments to the accomplishments of man. The distant slave songs in the mid-morning fields carried my thoughts to the Pyramids.

Van Gogh's Slice

By Taryn L. Hook

I am bloody and naked underneath Vincent van Gogh. The glint in his eyes reflects the steel glint in the straight edged razor he brandishes above my head. His gnashed teeth are perfect canvasses of revenge. With a banshee-like wail, he thrusts the flesh-encrusted blade towards my neck.

* * *

Only hours before--and four hundred years in the future--, I stood in Duff's office awaiting my next Harvester's Mission. Duff wore a shiny Hologram Patch over his right eye, his accompanying Holo-Mouth displaying rows of sooty teeth.

I turn away from Duff's Holo-Mouth, complete with 18th century pirate's breath, spewing into my face. Instead, I concentrate on dozens of Relics in display shelves on the left wall, each encased in red laser glass--ready for the Harvester's Guild highest bidder. Coveted items such as saints' fingers, martyrs' excrement, and royal organ fluids, resting on mounds of purple silk.

"Do you know, Kalista?" asks Duff, "why I chose this Holo-Mouth and costume today? Hardy. Har. Har." Duff, though short and smashed looking, always manages to appear taller when celebrating a successful Harvester's Mission.

"Because Catch and Jetler brought back a peg-leg and an ancient bottle of rum from the Blackbeard expedition, rather than Blackbeard's actual severed head?"

Duff's bushy eyebrows bunch together in a Jupiter Caterpillar unibrow. "Don't be fresh with me, young lady. Remember, you're just a zlick away from your Uncle Zefron's fate. One zlick away from having your own head stuck on a Metacadmun Pole, in the City Square, for all to gawk at 'til the end of time. You don't want to be Zefronated, do you?" he says with extra emphasis on the "Z." "You're not hoping to

45

'roll' as his head did, are you?" At this, Duff erupts into such a herky-jerky fit of "Hardy. Har. Hars," intermittently mixed with "Aaarghs," I think he might choke on his own spit.

I always vow never to let Duff's Uncle Zefron jokes upset me, but they always do. We Harvesters are the most elite time travelers in the Post Climate Modulation Society. That I, niece of the infamous Jackson Zefron, was chosen as a Candidate for Full Harvester status was extraordinary. However, the Guild hardly had a choice, since the applicant who scores the highest on the entrance exam is guaranteed admittance to the Harvester's Academy--and I scored the highest. Still, Duff, as well as my fellow Harvester Candidates, never let me forget the fact that I was "Zefron's Progeny." There were the constant bad jokes, name-calling, and more recently, a stinging rhyme that Catch, Jetler, and the other Candidates constantly repeated:

"Jackson Zefron went back in time
Back to collect John the Baptist's head
But he cheated and cut it off himself instead
Because of his criminal act, he got the axe
Now his head is stuck on a Metacadmun pole for all to see,
Kryptoplasticized forever in ignominy..."

As I stare at the arm of some sixteenth century saint in the display cabinet, I try not to think of Uncle Zefron's preserved head in the City Square, impaled on that indifferent Metacadmun stake, his long grey hair blowing in the nuclear winds. Instead, I say with convincing gusto, "Forgive my insolence, Master Duff. I know you're celebrating because Catch and Jetler succeeded in their Mission. I'm certain such a prized Relic as Blackbeard's head will create a bidding war amongst the Harvester's Guild members."

Duff's drooling Holo-Teeth grin in a funny U-shape so that the ends of his lips almost touch his round, flushed cheeks. "That's better, Kalista. That's what I like to see. A good attitude. An optimistic outlook." Duff limps around me on his fake peg leg. "Catch and Jetler did indeed come back from their Mission with Target Blackbeard's head. It tested completely pure. Not a trace of their LeptonDNA was found on the Relic. Their Seedset recordings also showed that they in no way influenced or manipulated Blackbeard's beheading. As the historical records we have left indicate, Target Blackbeard was killed by his enemy Maynard, whose crew then cut off his head. Catch and Jetler blended in perfectly with these scallywags, and, at the exact moment Blackbeard was decapitated, they caught his head in their expandable Relic Net--a perfect Mission. You could learn a lot from those two, Kalista."

"You mean like how to be total arrogant assholes?" I think, staring again at the display case, this time toward a cluster of hair strands protruding from a tiny patch of skullcap. A Relic harvested when it fell off the body of the 16th century peasant discovered wrapped in the Shroud of Turin.

Duff's mouth curls in a piratey smirk. "You know, Kalista, a Harvester..."

"A Harvester is only as good as his 'target's pure flesh,'" I finish. "To maintain the 'purity' of a Relic, a Harvester must never cut off a body part from a Target himself. Separations of body parts and other organic matter, such as bodily fluids, must occur in manners consistent with the historical record as we know it. Additionally, the Relic must be untainted by the Harvester's smallest known DNA particle, LeptonDNA."

So sensitive and fragile is LeptonDNA that just passing one's hand over a prospective Relic can result in contamination, thus making it un-marketable to the Guild--not to mention the harsh punishment doled out to Harvesters who break this rule. Again, I try not to think of my Uncle Zefron's fate.

"Hardy, Har, Har." Duff pats his stretched belly. "That's correct, Kalista. You can be disobedient and stubborn, young lady, but, I must admit, you do possess intelligence, as well as spunk and courage, which is why I have chosen you for a most special, unique, and daring assignment. If you pull this one off, any remaining doubts Guild members might have about your loyalty and integrity because of your Uncle Zefron's crime will be eliminated."

"What is the Mission, Sir?" Duff doesn't answer. Instead, he stomp-pegs across the marble floor, pacing back and forth, his Holo-Mouth now oozing Holo-Tobacco mixed with stringy strands of Holo-Saliva. Harvester's Hell. He was now going to lecture me about the Harvester's

History and Creed. Geez. For the umpteenth time.

"Do you know the origins of our esteemed organization, the Harvester's Galaxy-Wide Guild, Kalista?"

"Yes, Sir, I-"

"When time travel was developed in the Post Climate Modulation Period, we were able to confirm there were an infinite number of past dimensions. This, of course, meant there were an infinite number of opportunities for repeat visits back to any one of an infinite number of Time Quadrants. The permutations were limitless. At any given moment, any time-travel scumbag wannabe could go back in time ad nauseam. There was no regulation." Stomp. Stomp of Duff's peg leg. "No regulation at all on how many trips someone could make back into time. It was a disaster. Thousands traveled back to the 21st Century, before the mass destruction caused by Climate Modulation. There, they stole all of the priceless art, gold, and gems they could get their hands on--items lost in the chaos of Climate Modulation and unavailable in today's 23rd Century. And do you know what happened as a result, Kalista?" Duff stopped peg stomping for a moment to face me, his tobacco saliva flowing even gummier than before. "The market was flooded with items that used to be priceless, because they were one-of-a kind, or because they were extremely rare. As a result, market prices were driven down to practically nothing." Duff shook his head like a pirate shaking lice out of his greasy hair. At one time, there were thousands of *Mona Lisas* around and even more Hope Diamonds. You could buy original Monets, Picassos, and Rembrandts for less than the price of a Thrat hot dog."

"Sir, sorry to interrupt, but I know all about-"

"And that's why the Harvester's Guild was established, Kalista. The first government agency to establish strict controls over time travel. There had to be standards, Goddammit. Standards, Kalista. As I just explained, art and jewels were now worthless. However, due to the new, tightened restrictions on time travel, one class of items suddenly became priceless. Presently, the most expensive, rarest, and sought after items in the Galaxy. The Relics we Harvesters collect for the Guild."

"Body parts of historically famous people, Sir."

The stringy saliva transforms into a frothy foam sticking to the outer corners of Duff's Holo-Lips. "Yes, Kalista. Yes!" Duff unsheathes a small dagger from his belt, waving it irhythmically in the air. "Yes." Stab. Stab. "Yes, Kalista." Blunt stab. "Body parts of famous people. Only we Harvesters are licensed by the Guild to collect such incredible Relics, and in extremely limited quantities so the market will not be flooded as beforehand. We are prohibited from separating Relics from our Target's bodies ourselves, of course. The separation must occur by some natural, documented, historical event--like an execution, natural disaster, accident or a murder, to name just a few possible ways a Relic can be obtained. And when those body parts--or fluids--fall, we are there to catch them in our Relic Nets, like Blackbeard's head, for example." Swish. Stab. "We Harvesters are the best. The brightest. The most...ethical individuals." Duff averts his patchless left eye on this last expression. Whenever he gets to the ethical part of the Harvester's Creed, he never looks at me. In turn, this always makes my own thoughts contemplate Zefron once again.

My Uncle Zefron was one of the first Harvesters to collect Relics from the ancient world. He brought back Saint Agatha's breasts, cut off by a Roman Prefect. Fresh blood from Abel. And even the Harvester's Holy Grail--a piece of Christ's liver, ejected from his body when Longinus's lance plunged into his side.

He was rich, famous, and widely admired for bringing back only the purest of Relics. This is why no one thought anything remarkable would happen when Zefron was assigned to Harvest John the Baptist's head. But, nevertheless, something remarkable did happen. For my Uncle Zefron apparently broke the cardinal Harvester's Creed by tainting the Relic.

His Seedset betrayed him. Seedsets are injected under a Harvester's skin just above the right wrist. They are time travel devices, but also serve another purpose and function. As audio and video recorders, Seedsets saturate Harvesters' bodies with nano recorders, thus documenting every moment of a given Harvester's Mission. And Zefron's Seedset clearly recorded him cutting off John the Baptist's head instead of following protocol by leaving the job to Herod's executioners, as documented in the historical record.

And that's why Zefron paid the Harvester's ultimate price. What he took from John the Baptist, the Guild took from him-- his head. Hung in the City Square, right next to the head of the incompetent Harvester who contaminated Marie Antoinette's execution by pulling the guillotine lever himself.

Some explained Zefron's actions by speculating that he stayed in the past longer than the established 10-hour maximum, contracting time travel psychosis as a result. Others believed he was burned out and on a suicide mission, planning all along to get caught and executed. But I have a different theory. Because Uncle Zefron had enemies who envied his successes, I always believed they rigged his Seedset. I couldn't prove it, of course. And, in the end, it didn't really matter what the zlick happened. Uncle Zefron was still dead and, because of guilt by association, my actions as a Harvester's Candidate were overly scrutinized. But, I would prove all the doubters wrong. I would succeed. Then no one would dare make tasteless jokes or repeat nasty rhymes ever again. Especially after I earned a place in the Harvester's Hall of Fame.

"Sir. The special assignment you mentioned?" I tried to disguise the waver in my voice that Duff would most certainly recognize as emotional hunger. "Whatever it is. Whatever Time Quadrant you want to send me to... no matter how dangerous. I'm in. All in."

Duff's pirate teeth flickered, as if there was a momentary interference in the current linking his Holo-Molars. "Hardy. Har. Har, Kalista. You'll need balls bigger than a Martian Polar Bear. For, you'll be Harvesting one of the most popular Relics of the year. Black holes above, it is hot, hot, hot. Coveted by the wealthiest Guild members. The famous Post-Impressionist painter, Vincent van Gogh's ear." Duff twirled the right end of his coal colored moustache into a tiny twisty-tip.

"But, sir. I thought Jax and Planter were covering that Mission."

Duff almost twisted the end of his moustache right off. "Er...um...they ran into some difficulties, Kalista. Some...obstacles."

"Did they contaminate the Relic?"

Duff cleared his throat in a staccato way. "No. No. Nothing like that.

The Relic is pure and the timeline uncompromised. They were overworked, that's all. Which contributed to their--er--inability to Harvest Target van Gogh's Relic. Therefore, the Guild, graciously granted them some much needed re-education. Er…I mean rest at the Centaurus A Harvester Rehabilitation Center." Duff--or rather his grit and slime-covered teeth--smiled broadly at me. "Forget about Jax and Planter, Kalista, we need to concentrate on you now. To prepare for the Mission, you'll be dressed as a maid servant; one from the nearby village of Arles, France. This is the town, as you know, where the Target van Gogh resided before his…his…"

"Before he cut his ear off in a fit of madness on December 13, 1888 and presented it to a prostitute," I finished. "I've read all about it in the Harvester's Grand Library."

"Yes, Kalista. That's how we believe Target van Gogh mutilated himself, although the exact historical details are murky, as you no doubt found from your studies. Many details of van Gogh's life story were lost during the Climate Modulation Wars. In any event, the plan to Harvest the Target's ear is this: you will materialize via your Seedset in front of van Gogh's bedroom door at 10pm on December 12, 1888. Identify yourself as a maid sent by his brother, Theo, to bring him his evening soup. We believe he cut off his ear early the next morning, most likely between 1am and 6am. However, since we do not know exactly how or when the event occurred, you'll need to use all your wit, intelligence, and subterfuge skills to gain van Gogh's trust, ascertaining exactly what happened. Then, it's your job to be close to him at the exact moment he cuts off his ear. This way it can drop ever so neatly into your sterile Relic Net, remaining pure flesh."

"I've got it covered, Sir."

"Good girl. But remember, to prevent time travel psychosis, you'll only have ten hours to complete your Harvest before your Seedset implant will automatically transport you back to our present Time Quadrant."

"I promise to make you proud, Sir," I said. "Whatever obstacles Jax and Planter faced in 1888, I'll overcome them. The Guild will have its precious Relic."

* * *

I stand in front of a pine wood door, barely five feet tall, and not more than three feet wide. Fortunately, I know beforehand exactly what's inside this room located within van Gogh's yellow-as-a-canary house in Arles, the South of France, for I had carefully studied his painting entitled, "Bedroom in Arles." In fact, over the last three days, I only left my pod at the Harvester's Grand Library once, having immersed myself in the file entitled "Post Climate Modulation: Surviving Van Gogh Works." The painting, "Bedroom in Arles," is widely believed to depict the room van Gogh occupied at the time he sliced off part of his ear. And, although the precise circumstances of his self-mutilation have been lost to time, present historians believe the event occurred in or near that Arles bedroom.

From studying van Gogh's painting, I sense that behind this sparse wooden entrance exists a room in which the skewed walls itch for a chance to cave in on its clinically depressed occupant. A narrow bed that doesn't look big enough for a malnourished child. A stifling window. A lonely chair. Van Gogh's empty last days reflected in a poetic-painting of his isolated existence.

During this time period, near the end of his life, van Gogh was rumored to be practically an invalid. I imagine his wrinkled hands as they somehow manage to slice off his grey, shriveled ear. How easy it would be to Harvest the fleshy prize as it fell, from van Gogh's trembling blade into my sterile Relic Net. Mission accomplished. My salvation from the legacy of Zefronation would be complete as a result.

Still, with such a light assignment, I can't help but wonder where Jax and Planter might have gone wrong. I knew them to be amongst the most competent and promising Harvester Candidates. Yet, Duff informed me they never even came close to seeing van Gogh during their Mission. Where had they failed? Duff seemed particularly cagey and incredibly vague when I questioned him on the particulars. Caution was obviously in order.

With a firm, but delicate hand, I rap lightly on van Gogh's Lilliputian door. "It's Antoinette from the village sent to bring you your evening soup, Monsieur Van Gogh." I don't care for the sound of my voice. It reminds me of the high-pitched wails of the Anoevirus-infected cats circling Zefron's impaled head at midnight. *"Don't let your desire to avenge your family name transform into a case of nerves, Kalista. You never get nervous. It's one of your greatest strengths. Try again. You can do better."*

This time my voice is timid yet smooth. More characteristic of a young servant girl native to the region and Time Quadrant. Again, no answer. And yet, I detect distinct noises emerging from that anemic room. How strange. Laughter. A man's laugh, mixed with the giggling of a woman. A titanium beam-like laugh. The kind of steady, full-bodied laughter one would expect from a healthy man, appropriately reacting to a silly joke told by some teasing child-woman.

Perhaps I'm at wrong room. In the wrong house. Perhaps even in the wrong Time Quadrant. It's happened before. Seedset time travel, for all its hype, isn't perfect. As I muse on the possibility that Duff messed this one up, I hear a whoosh, like a steel blade carving the air in half. A squishy noise of direct contact--like hard metal thrashing plump flesh. I wait for the terrible scream that is sure to follow, but hear instead, a moan of...pleasure?

"You little devil," intones the man. "Come to Papa, Moncherie. Come here right now before I peel more skin off that skinny frame. Believe me when I say it does not look like you have much more buttocks to spare." Deep laughter mixed with hypersonic giggling again.

I knock again, louder this time. The laughter stops. A deep voice says, "Enter." Carefully, very carefully, I open the door. It creaks loudly, and I start clicking my front teeth together. Harvester's Hell! *"Don't blow this one, Kalista. Don't self-fulfill everyone's expectations that you'll end up just like your Uncle Zefron."* My thoughts turn to this year's Harvester's Ursa Triangular Ball. Everyone receives a gift from the other Candidates. Catch and Jetler convinced all my fellow Candidates to pitch in for mine. Oh, joy of joys. A newly minted Metacadmun Stake complete with a plot of land accompanying an eternal deed right next to Zefron's Kryptoplasticized head. *"Reserved Just For You, With Greatest Affection,"* read the accompanying plaque. *"Make sure those assholes wasted their money, Kalista. Make sure,*" I tell myself.

I quickly survey the room, memorizing every detail. This bedroom is nothing like the cramped, rickety lodgings depicted in the van Gogh archives at the Harvester's Grand Library. I would even say it approaches grand for the times. A creamy chair sporting a silken seat covered in red and white stripes, intermingled with yellow fleur de lises, echoing the pattern of the heavy silk tasseled drapes partially covering two arched windows leading to a balcony. A ceiling to floor length mirror rests against the far wall, bordered by golden maidens and dancing cherubs gathering water from a woodsy well, their long locks only partially covering their amply nude bodies.

However, it was the bed occupying the center of the kingly suite that grabbed my attention the most. Not a skinny cot from the painting at all, but rather a massive four-poster bed complete with yellow silk sheets and velvet burgundy pillows. Looming in a kind of three-dimensional magnificence over the bed was the headboard--a snarling lion's head carved from cherry wood, replete with six-inch canines.

In the middle of the bed, reclines a petite woman with ebony locks hanging well past her waist, her eyes bluer than Uranus sandstone. She doesn't move an inch when I enter, but simply regards me as if strangers regularly enter this bedroom. One dainty hand partially covers rosy blushed lips--lips smiling ever so slightly as if reflecting on a private joke still lingering in the perfumed air.

A zlick later, the soup is knocked from my hands by a blunt force from behind. As the warm liquid spatters, Jackson Pollock-style, onto the granite floor, a massive hand wraps around my throat. Clearly, with one minor flick of the wrist, these particular hands could break my neck. I must remain calm and, at all costs, retain my Cover. That is one of the Cardinal Harvester's Rules: "Maintain one's Cover no matter what one might have to do."

"Sir. Sir," I manage to gasp in my best French. "Please don't hurt me. Perhaps I have foolishly stumbled into the wrong room."

"You bet you have the wrong room," the man says, spewing hot breath laced with alcohol and tobacco. The stench curls around my neck, up my face, and into my nostrils. The man whirls me around, shoving me across the room, then slams me onto the bed. I look up into green eyes, iridescent as the Martian Jade Stones that Duff uses for paperweights. Next, I notice his mouth. Not like sickly, thin wires depicted in van Gogh's self-portraits, which I had also studied, but full and rich instead. Robust lips sucking on a fat brown cigar, surrounded by a ruddy red beard and moustache. I observe his ears. They fit his head so perfectly. They look Michelangeloish even. Not at all like the dried prunes depicted in the library archives.

Every feature matches van Gogh's self-portraits, but in an overblown, anything but wasting away type of manner. Thin and frail are not even in his universe. Lacking is an aura of a mentally ill individual on the brink of self-mutilation. Every muscle in his unexpectantly wide face screams self-assurance, pride, and a particular inner resolve. Even the way his cigar hangs from his mouth defies gravity, spits in the face of any hint of self-despair. It looks incredibly solid, like it will never fall from his lips, even through earthquakes, floods, and hurricanes.

"Look at her, Marie!" he laughs, nodding in my direction, "I think this little slip of a girl is another one of them. There is just something not right about her. I don't know what it is, but…" He buries his nose in my cleavage "… she smells funny just like the others. I thought them gone for good after the last two imbeciles. Yet, they--whomever they are-- were stupid enough to send another." He presses his naked un-van Gogh-like body against mine, takes a puff on his cigar, and unfurls wood against my leg. He rips my white servant girl's cap off my head, sniffing my hair like an overeager dung Thrat. "You are one of them, aren't you, wench?"

I burst into tears and talk very rapidly. "I do not know this 'them' to which you are referring. I am a simple servant girl sent by Monsieur Theo van Gogh to serve his brother, Monsieur Vincent van Gogh, soup. Might you be Monsieur Vincent van Gogh, kind sir, or might you know where I can find him?" Giggles. Lots of giggles from Marie, still naked-nestled in the rumpled silk sheets.

"You know I am he, bitch. That is why you are here." He grabs me by the back of my head, and shoves my face downward where I find myself directly in line with his penis, also quite Michelangeloish. Next, he pulls me upwards and begins to trace a circle with it on my leg. "Am I not even more handsome than you envisioned...in every conceivable way?" He then proceeds to compose an expansive wide-leaf Sunflower on my thigh. Swirling, curling petals finished by a spray of dew soaking my leg. Afterwards, his low, panting growls remind me of an extinct Pre-Climate Modulation grizzly bear.

His bearish exhaustion complete, he asks, "Do you need any more proof that I," he looks between his legs and smiles, "am Vincent van Gogh in the flesh, Pretty Morsel. That is what I will call you, I think. My Pretty Morsel. Your masters sent two of your colleagues before you to assassinate me, both of them ugly and ignorant. Nevertheless, I was not surprised. Many ignorant people want me dead, including my brother Theo who believes I shame the family with my "unconscionable antics." And then there is my rival Gauguin who is insanely jealous of my talent to the point of sheer distraction. Not to mention the French government for inflicting my "lewd art" on the masses.

He once again tightens his grip around my throat. "Which one? Which one of these sent you? Tell me Pretty Morsel." He shakes me-- hard. I look up at him with wide eyes. "Monsieur, please. I know nothing about the matters of which you speak."

He regards me for a few moments, then releases his grip somewhat. "Well, at least this time they had the common sense to send a woman. And a hell of a good looking one at that." It's as if his broad smile stimulates his hormones, and, like the extinct grizzly bear he reminds me of, spews a musky scent from some unknown orifice. "Beautiful blonde hair. Mmm. Like shafts of wheat waving in an Arles storm. Eyes the color of irises. Skin like a pail of fresh, creamy milk."

He picks up a straight edged razor from the bedside table. Ever so slowly, he traces it around the outline of my right ear, which starts to bleed, then licks the blood trail. "MMM. Like honey." This time, he traces the outline of my chin with the edge of the blade. "Since you refuse to reveal your identity or that of your Masters,' I now offer you two choices. Join Marie and me in my yellow lust den for the evening..." He lifts his eyes to the ceiling "...or join your impotent predecessors." I follow his gaze. There, arranged, in a flower-like pattern are body parts nailed to the oak rafters. A decaying foot linked by a rope to four half-skeletized feet and legs. Poppies in a vase by any other name. So Jax and Planter are at the Centaurus A Rehabilitation Center. I don't think so.

"Beautiful, isn't it?" says van Gogh. "I have no idea where each of their right arms went, though. It's quite a mystery which vexes me to no end, for it's as if those limbs disappeared into thin air. However, no matter. I certainly have enough material with which to work." He begins to laugh again.

That asshole. That stinking bastard Duff obviously did not tell me the truth about Jax and Planter's prior Mission to Harvest van Gogh's ear. Oh, he screwed me over big time. It all made horrifying sense now. Jax and Planter's Seedsets were calibrated to transport them back to the 23rd century after ten hours. However, because their Seedsets were embedded in their right arms, only these limbs were transported back to Duff. The rest of their bodies, chopped up by van Gogh, were being made into macabre sunflowers on his ceiling. Jax and Planter's grisly end would have been recorded by their Seedsets and reviewed by Duff. And that stupid asshole Duff, as my Overseer, was obligated to reveal all of this to me. Regulations state I was owed full disclosure about prior failed missions. That way, I would be prepared to face the murderous van Gogh. But, Duff revealed none of these facts to me, and I think I knew why.

Duff and his Guild cronies knew that few, if any, Harvesters would accept such a Mission if they knew the true facts about Jax and Planter's fate. And, anyway, why waste a perfectly good Harvester on a perilous mission if you have an expendable one to send first? Before risking anyone else, why not send the one Candidate who no one would make too much of a fuss over if she was killed in action? Everyone expected her to fail at some point anyway just like her Uncle did. *Zefron's progeny*. Me.

But there is one thing in the equation that Duff forgot. I am a survivor. When I get back home, I'll shove Duff's peg leg down his throat--after I hand him van Gogh's pure, amputated ear. I'll do whatever I must to ensure this Mission is a complete success. Take that, Duff, you stupid Thrat's ass.

I shove myself against van Gogh's naked torso, causing him to raise an eyebrow. "Alright Monsieur van Gogh." I try to giggle like Marie. But, I'm not used to giggling. More like chugging vats of Pluton Ale, which makes my giggle sound more like that than flirting. "I'll do whatever you want." This time I sound a little sweeter, more like the honey with which van Gogh says my blood is infused. The subterfuge tactic works, and he releases his grip on my wrists. Good. If he believes I'm young and dumb, then I'll have a better chance at ultimately gaining my prize--and my glory.

He throws his head back. "Hah. Hah. Hah. Excellent choice, Pretty Morsel." He then pulls me farther up onto the silken sheets, positioning me right next to the now almost hysterically laughing Marie. Still with the smoldering cigar hanging from his mouth, he guzzles from a bottle of absinthe, wiping his mouth with the back of his Orangutan-like hand.

"Oh, my Pretty Morsel." He draws a long puff on the fat cigar, expelling two streams of smoke through his nostrils, then once again glances up at the grotesque coils of decaying body parts plastered to the ceiling. "They drip," he says. "They drip in many colors, but red is the prevalent palette." Another deep puff. "That is why this absinthe is crimson instead of clear." He raises his bottle. "I drink to your predecessors...and I also drink them. How do you like that, Pretty Morsel?"

Without a word, I grab the bottle from his hand and take a giant swig. "Mmmm. Like red licorice, Monsieur van Gogh."

Van Gogh's cigar does not look so secure this time, and I think it's actually in danger of falling and singeing his genitals. He claps slowly. "Touché, my Pretty Morsel. Touché. Now, show me a painting. Bring heaven to my realm and mix it with art." He gestures at Marie. "Show me my next inspiration, Mon Cheries. He laughs and takes another puff, then a swig. "Hurry now. No man can wait an eternity for paradise."

I notice darkness creeping behind the tasseled curtains partially covering the French doors to the patio. From reviewing my Seedset Eye Clock, I estimate that van Gogh will likely slice off a chunk of his left ear in approximately five to seven hours from now, in the early morning. And, no matter his machismo, arrogance, or seeming confidence, I will collect it, catching it in my Relic Net, which is safely tucked away in its tiny, camouflaged sack underneath my wrist. No matter what type of humiliation I am forced to endure, I will collect Target van Gogh's ear. No matter the cost.

And so, I slip off my dress and throw it on the floor. Marie and I begin to kiss, tongues twisting, while van Gogh reclines against the headboard of the alive-looking lion alternately swigging his absinthe and puffing his cigar. He watches our every move before grabbing a brush from the bedside table, then dipping it in a can filled with red ochre. He paints strange flourishes on the chrome yellow wall above the headboard. Some of his strokes are wavy lines, others more like the signs of infinity. Still others are simple, interlocking circles. Marie and I are to make love in "naked whirls," he orders, just like his "musings on the wall."

Accordingly, we copy what he paints. The tip of my tongue forms infinity signs on Marie's warm breasts. Next, her teeth nibble circles of bliss around my areolas. In addition, we both use our tongues, lips, and fingertips to emulate his wavy lines between each other's inner thighs.

Then, van Gogh dumps yellow paint on our bellies and we crash and grind into each other, splashing around as if caught in an errant ocean wave. "My brother Theo says my paintings are unsellable," says van Gogh. "One cannot even give away the 'dense, clotted, murky,' things I paint, claims Theo, who fancies himself an art dealer. However, this is because Theo does not possess inspiration. And his clients lack any semblance of the notions of beauty and salvation. Not as I do anyway. For none of them are gazing right now, upon you two cherubs, you two who meld holy paint with sacrosanct skin, paving my way to redemption."

Next, as if possessed by a demon, he is upon us both. Not a shell of a man, with a stick neck and sickly pea soup pallor, as depicted in his self-portraits. But an engulfing force, an energy-sucking black hole, massive enough to devour us both in one supreme gulp.

There isn't much in the way of concrete description that I can remember about the rest of that night, except that everything about it was the most concrete thing I've ever experienced, have ever felt. My memories are murky, yet as vivid as the two blazing suns on the planet

Croesus, a vision I'm sure van Gogh would paint with obsession.

Yet, there are some things I do remember clearly. The tastiest, thirstiest, most desperately tingly things. The sound of dry wheat brushing against wet grass. Golden sunflowers transforming into flushed, plump carnations. His full mouth blowing my petals, which mimic responsive blooms in the Arles sun on a spring day. Marie's folded, swollen lips on his bristly bearded ones.

At some point amidst the blood and paint, I remember his arms flapping. As if he was one of the black boomerang crows, scars against the landscape, from his masterpiece, "Wheatfield with Crows." Like his crows, he seemingly flies through the air, and then plunges deep inside me. Oh so deep on a blue-black night, oh so many centuries ago. Yet still only hours from my upcoming 23rd Century Waterloo. And the entire time as I moan, the star-swollen heavens shine above. Stars like pinwheels, brighter than the moon, more illuminated than the sun. Cartwheeling across the sky in swooshing, blurring patterns, as he alternatively cartwheels inside of us two. Bright, colliding centers, expanding outwards. Forever outwards. Then down, inside-out,--and up again--into the cool, sated evening of our pleasure.

And then there is van Gogh's straight edged razor--his alternate paintbrush. This I remember all too well, as my body still bears its mark. I hear Marie's hysterical girl laugh as his razor, illuminated by flickering candles in all its dried flesh-chunked glory, cuts a masterpiece in her back. A bas-relief of connected, curling orbs paying homage to his lust for life. To his never ending search for redemption from boredom and fear of a colorless existence.

After carving Marie's back, my tongue follows the bloody grooves up to her maiden white shoulders. After I am finished, van Gogh kisses Marie's back, her gushing blood darkening his red beard even more. Gushing like an ancient Roman fountain into his open mouth. When it is my turn to be painted, he takes a more symmetric approach, etching delicate irises onto my stomach, drip...drip...dripping into sunny colored bed sheets.

Afterwards, in the sea of blood, we three hold hands and laugh as if we only had hours to live. At that moment, I am not a Harvester. Not a time traveler. Marie and I are mortal offerings to van Gogh's immutable vision of paradise. Arcs and curves, and circles. So many shapes to comprehend. To explore. To understand. Until nothing matters anymore. Nothing. Except the three of us. And the very last thing I remember before we fall asleep in each other's arms, are his words: "Ahhh, that was a Starry Night indeed. One I shall be compelled to paint. One that will shake the world of all who become fortunate enough to gaze upon its splendor."

* * *

In the morning, the atmosphere is somewhat stark and charcoal, much like van Gogh's early minimalist works. The sheets and walls are somehow not so vibrantly yellow, the red stains not so vitally full of life. Rather, they possess a sad, maroon-caked cast. The sheets are rough, too, their once smooth silkiness marred with the crustiness of dried blood intermingled with bits of flesh.

My absinthe-infested eyes are a bit blurry, and too late do I see Target Vincent van Gogh above me, swinging his effervescently red razor blade towards my neck. "I will get rid of you nuisances once and for all. For starry nights always fade into the desperation of morning, and so shall you. I WILL add you to my collection, my Pretty Little Morsel, just like your foolhardy predecessors who grace my ceiling." Like a guillotine, the blade falls heavy. But, my daily routine at the Harvester's 24 Hour Anti-Grav Gym has made my reflexes sharp. I roll to the side just as the blade is buried next to my head, slicing through the crusty silk.

I grab van Gogh's arm, still grasping the blade, as we struggle. Meanwhile, Marie, with a petite smile on her petite face, sleeps soundly. Van Gogh manages to hoist himself up against the headboard. Once pressed against the lion's jutting teeth, he raises the blade up yet again. His bare feet, however, lacking traction on an area of the sheets still wet with assorted bodily fluids, cause him to slip, and he careens downwards, as if on a slide. He then drops the blade, while attempting to regain his position. Unfortunately, for van Gogh, the blade lands right into my open hand, and as he slides by my hand, I accidentally slice most of his left ear off. His liberated ear then bounces off the right canine of the headboard lion and into my open mouth.

Harvester's Hell, I am ruined. For, intentional or not, I have broken the Harvester's Creed in multiple ways. Just like my Uncle Zefron allegedly cut off John the Baptist's head, I cut off van Gogh's ear instead of allowing the natural course of historical events to unfold. My Seedset will have recorded this illegal action. I'm screwed in another way as well. The Harvester's Guild Lab will detect the LeptonDNA from my mouth contaminating the Relic.

I notice the shock in van Gogh's widened eyes at the same time he sees the desperate, lost look in mine. At this point, the Seedset in my arm buzzes, signaling that my allocation in this Time Quadrant is nearly over. I want to stay longer. To fix this mess. Nevertheless, there is only enough time for me to grab my dress from the floor and pull it over my head before I am transported back to the 23rd Century, still with van Gogh's mangled earlobe sticking out of my white lipped mouth.

* * *

I am wet and shivering in a fetal position, like a puddle of ionized Jell-O, on Duff's Italian Marble floor. Quickly, I pull my Relic Net out of my wrist skin bag and stuff van Gogh's ear into it. Then I pass out, suffering from a case of Harvester's Sickness, common amongst time travelers. When I awake, the Relic Net is no longer in my hand. Instead, something hovers in front of my blurred eyes. Teeth. Oh, no! I'm staring at Duff's Holo-Teeth, each one a miniature representation of van Gogh's greatest paintings - sunflowers, cypress trees, and whirling stars in a whirling sky. I start to gag. Surely, by now, Duff has reviewed my Seedset recording and tested the Relic for purity. I am so totally doomed. I've fulfilled everyone's expectations of me--I'm a failure, not fit to be a Harvester. Truly Zefron's progeny.

Barely lifting up my damp head, I see Duff wearing a painter's beret. His beard is dyed a cheap looking red, like the color the waitresses at the Galactic Whore House wear on their fingernails. Duff removes a paintbrush from his stained white painter's apron, tickling my nose with a short swirl. "Hmm. Some trip you had, I see, Kalista." I cringe. He smiles a much too gummy smile. Then, he points at his mouth. "Do you like the Holo-Teeth? A little something to welcome you home--and wish you a most well deserved congratulations.

"Congratulations?" I repeat. He's mocking me. Damn him. Just get it over with Duff, you lying, duplicitous bastard. But, know this. Before I end up next to Zefron, my head on a Metacadmun Pole, I'll have my revenge on you for sending me on a compromised mission--one you most certainly knew would end in disaster after learning of Jax and Planter's fate.

"Ah, Kalista. You're going to be a most famous Harvester. Yes, indeed. A celebrity even."

"Yeah," I think to myself, "but for all the wrong reasons." Duff orders me to stand up. "But, first, young lady, we have a serious matter to discuss." For several moments, I don't move from the cold marble floor. I can't move. Can't even breathe. Finally, I gather the strength to stand and face my accuser. Although I yearn to wring his neck until his Holo-Teeth fall out, I decide to try and reason with him first. Attempt to save my life using my gift of persuasion.

"Sir, I can explain."

No Holo-Teeth smile on Duff's face this time. Even his cheap red beard looks serious.

"The Guild Lab has determined that this whole debacle is not your fault, my dear."

"Not...my...fault?"

"Yes. It's not your fault that your Seedset was defective. I took the liberty of downloading your Seedset while you were out. It recorded nothing. Absolutely nothing of your mission. Just some blurry shapes that seemed to swirl around in circles or some such nonsense."

"So...you...don't know what happened?"

"No idea. However, you're in luck, Kalista. The Harvester's Guild unanimously voted that the Relic could be ruled pure even without your Seedset recording. But only if Target van Gogh's ear was not contaminated with your LeptonDNA."

I stiffen. Here it comes. Harvester's Hell. Zefron, I'll be joining you soon.

"Sir. I'm begging you. Let me explain."

"Explain what, Kalista? The Relic has been ruled clear. Totally uncontaminated." Duff barrels towards me. Behind his loose painter's apron, I can see his blubber wiggling as he gets nearer. I close my eyes and feel arms around my waist, squeezing me like I am the long, lost prodigal daughter. Then, SMACK, Duff plants sticky, wet kisses all over my mortified cheeks. "Kalista, my dearest Kalista. My sweet girl. Congratulations. Never again will your name be mentioned in the same sentence as Zefron's. But, more importantly, I am going to be rich...I mean...er... we are going to be rich. The bidding war has already begun in the Guild. One of the highest priced wars ever." Duff takes his black felt painter's cap off and plants it on my head. "And, it's because of you, Kalista. You!"

"It's really true, Sir. No LeptonDNA contamination?"

"Of course not, my dear. The Relic is certified pure by the Lab. The only way. The ONLY way the results could be incorrect would be if..." He throws his hand down as if swatting a fly out of the way. "Forget it..."

"How, Sir? Please finish. How could the lab be wrong?"

Duff laughs and waves his hand again. "It's so ridiculous, Kalista. I'm embarrassed to tell you. And I have no idea why you're so interested. You should be drunk on Antimatter Champagne right now. However, I'm in such a good mood, I will tell you.

If you, young lady, were a direct descendant of van Gogh's, then your LeptonDNA and van Gogh's would be a perfect match. You see, Seedset LeptonDNA tests are only designed to measure contamination of objects from the DNA of a biologically unrelated individual. The Guild never deemed it necessary to calibrate Seedsets in order to identify direct descendants of Targets. There was some discussion about adding this feature, but it was rejected due to the additional time and high costs involved. Also, no one believed that such a scenario would ever occur, because the projected likelihood was deemed to be so infinitesimally small. In other words, should you and van Gogh be close relatives, the Seedset would have no mechanism to differentiate your

LeptonDNA from his. Consequently, we wouldn't be able to ascertain if Target van Gogh's Relic was actually contaminated or not."

He winks. At the same time, his Holo-Teeth seem to wink. "In any event, we both know from studying van Gogh's life, or what we know of it, that such a scenario is for all intents and purposes impossible." He pats his painter's vest covering his bulging belly. "Van Gogh had no children. Of course, there were rumors but they are unsubstantiated."

"Rumors, Sir." I manage to utter. "What rumors?"

"Surely, Kalista, you, as one of our best students of history, know the story to which I am referring. The one in which van Gogh had an affair with a local girl...or prostitute. Reported to have had his child after a wild tryst, on which he actually based his most famous painting "The Starry Night." Ah, but this version of history was entirely rejected by mainstream historians. And, even if it were true, there's no way you could be related to this unknown woman's baby, now is there Kalista? You'd have to be her great, great, great and so-on, granddaughter. Besides, you didn't see any woman with van Gogh, did you, Kalista, on your Mission?"

"No Sir. There was no woman with the Target van Gogh." I cough, clearing van Gogh's ear blood from my throat, and look directly into Duff's eyes. "No woman whatsoever."

Duff pats his distended belly again. "Of course there wasn't, Kalista. But, I am interested to hear the circumstances of how van Gogh mutilated his ear. And so is the Guild. However, all that can wait for your official report. Right now, it's a time for celebration. Oh Harvester's Heaven. This ear will fetch a pretty price.

"You're going to be one of the most celebrated Harvester's ever, Kalista. Starry, Starry Night indeed."

Before The Clock Strikes Six

By Justin Tate

A woman preps in a kitchen. Like a robot, her movements are both jittery and fluid from repetition. She reaches into cabinets with urgency, gathering oils, jars, utensils and cookware. Ladles and tongs rattle in her grasp. A package of flour slips, bursts and clouds the air. The refrigerator is emptied onto the counter, one item at a time, all in a row. She plucks a few spices from the rack, reconsiders, and brings down the complete set. Her eyes dart toward the huge grandfather clock in the living room. It is five minutes before five.

She surveys the ingredients scattered about the counter. There is no logic to the array, it is simply all that she can find. Tonight she is preparing a new recipe from an old book. Anything can happen.

The recipe calls for one-quarter teaspoon thyme, two teaspoons vinegar, a tablespoon of Ocean Essentials brand sea salt (with iodide, a necessary nutrient) and one bay leaf to simmer in boiling water. She is surprised to see a pot of water already on the stove, churning with excessive heat. She must have prepared it earlier and forgot. It is a strange thing to forget, but not inconceivable. After years of redundancy, some tasks can be completed without thought.

She removes a bay leaf from the spice rack and dangles it over the aluminum stockpot. She is reluctant to let it fall. The boiling water is tempestuous, heat bubbles popping and foam hissing around the edges. There is a morbid, murderous sensation as her fingers twist above the hellish current to release the herb. The bay leaf floats down like a feather, bobbing unevenly on the water's rough surface as it pulses with the waves. The recipe is unfamiliar and, by choosing it, she feels somewhat responsible—*guilty*—as the leaf's green sustenance bleeds out.

The grandfather clock chimes. She turns away from the scene—the bay leaf, the oceanic waters, the measuring spoons—and pauses to hear the hours toll. She visualizes the cogs, weights, spindles and springs ascending and descending behind the clock face. She sympathizes with

66

their life of infinite rotation. There is no levity in the chimes— ... *two ...
three ... four*—only duty.

 ... *Five ...*

The final reverberation shakes the kitchen with clamoring
dissonance. The clock is evil, she thinks. A dark mechanism designed to
overwhelm a room with its towering presence, its ticking and gonging,
reminding all that their pathetic lives cannot escape the circular loop of
a day. She fantasizes briefly about throwing the clock out—chopping it
into firewood with a sharp ax—before returning to the stove.

The boiling water is on the brink of bubbling over. She stirs it with a
wooden spoon and watches the bubbles momentarily abate before
springing to life again. There is something to be said about that, she
thinks. About the mysterious persistence of boiling water.

She wonders: is she more like the boiling water or the old wooden
spoon? Water—in its natural state—is docile and non-threatening. It
may be used to bring life to others but has few purposes for itself. If not
drunk, water may sit at the bottom of a well or drip in a cave. It may
decorate a spider's web or slosh down gutter drains. At best it may
flood and torment society. But eventually—when its time has come—
the sun will rise and turn all to vapor. What is left, if anything, will be a
worthless speck of salt—without iodide, a necessary nutrient.

Of course *boiling* water is different. Boiling water can kill if it wants.
It can melt human flesh or destroy the same weeds that suck up its soul.
It is powerful by nature and all must bend or dissolve to its authority.

She likes the allure of boiling water; the delicate entity that can
transform itself into a ruler. Still, she cannot quite compare herself to it.
It is too dominant. Too independent. She is more like well water or the
old wooden spoon: a utensil. Something used to serve somebody else.

She reduces the heat and picks up the book. She gazes at the recipe
for some time before realizing that the pages must have
turned. Fluttered, perhaps, by a breeze from the open window. The
recipe on the page is for blackberry pie which requires entirely different
ingredients and, moreover, there is already a blackberry pie cooling on
the windowsill, its form hidden behind stained curtains. She can smell
its lurid scent haunting the kitchen.

The pie's presence is a mystery. Did she bake it? Absent-mindedly preparing a pot of water may be possible, but an entire pie? Surely not.

She imagines herself standing zombie-like over the counter, blank-eyed and vacant, sifting flour, cutting butter, congealing berries, pre-heating, donning oven mitts and placing the pie on the windowsill to cool. It is too much. She refuses to believe it. She is forgetful and damaged, but her mind is still sharp.

And yet there is another concern: why blackberry? The last time she prepared a blackberry pie she had been punished. Why waste time on a forbidden dish? What would be her motive?

Wherever the pie came from, it must be tossed out.

She would dispose of it now except that she does not dare draw back the curtains to see if the pie actually exists.

Returning to the book, she tries again to find her place. It is a nice book, old and yellowed, with pencil renderings of each recipe. She cannot remember the title of the dish she is preparing and browses them all in hopes one will sound familiar. She turns and turns, but each recipe seems indefinitely right or distinctly wrong. The pie appears to be printed on every other page, as if sending a message.

As she reads, the grandfather clock fills the air with stagnant, impending doom. Bad things will happen when the clock strikes six. They always do. It is as expected as commercial breaks during a telecast. It is like—well, it is like clockwork.

Soon after the sixth chime, she will hear a car door slam followed by the sound of her husband's shoes on the pavement. His steps will be slow and calculated. He knows that she is under a deadline and thinks himself kind to give audible cues. He will jangle keys before inserting one into the lock. He will turn the lock so that it clangs. He will open the closet with a bang and grunt as he tucks away his briefcase. This will be his final warning.

The surprise will be how long it takes him to emerge from the hallway into the dining room. It could be thirty seconds or fifteen minutes. He varies this on purpose, she thinks, in attempt to catch her unprepared. If dinner is not served precisely to his tastes, he will beat her.

She learned this shortly after their honeymoon. A soup too cold, a soufflé too crisp, too many ice cubes or not enough—any minor mistake would be enough for him to strike. Over time she developed a vague understanding of his requirements, but there was always the chance that something unexpected would set him off.

The incident with the blackberry pie occurred on their sixth anniversary. She was determined to prepare a dessert that would prove herself worthy of him. He hit her, she believed, out of love and a desire to help her achieve. He wanted her to be perfect. She wanted that too. Housewife instincts told her that perfection could only be expressed through pie, so she spent the day picking fresh blackberries and isolated herself in the kitchen to concoct a masterpiece.

The problem was that her husband had, long ago during their short courtship, mentioned an allergy to blackberries. She had no recollection of this conversation and wondered if, in fact, he ever spoke of it. When he saw the pie he immediately interpreted the mistake as a violent act of disobedience. He accused her of trying to mock him, of wanting to collect insurance money, of desiring to leave him and engage in an illicit love affair.

Stunned, she had no time to react before being shoved to the tile, forehead smashing against the counter. He pinned her against the floor with one knee and twisted an arm behind her back. He roared accusations until her ears rang.

She tried to explain the misunderstanding, but her words came out as blubbering nonsense. Every time she sputtered he yanked her arm back further until it finally snapped. The sound was like tree branches in an ice storm. At first she was only shocked by his cruelty and then all she could think about was the pain. It roared through her arm, up her spine and into her brain. His knee grinded deeper into her back, pushing her face against the tile. The last thing she remembered before blacking out was having a fear that her neck would crack.

At some point he must have moved her. She woke sprawled out on the sofa, a pillow tucked awkwardly beneath her bruised scalp. The pain was full-bodied and heavy. She was too drowsy to move, so she slept. The clock woke her the following afternoon when it struck four. Her neck and back still hurt and her arm was limp, but she could move.

She sat upright on the sofa for several minutes, expressionless, watching the second hand on the clock loop round and round. It was only two hours before six. He would be home soon and he would be hungry.

If she ran away he would not be able to stop her. She could find refuge. She could survive. But if she stayed, there was the chance to make amends, to avoid being a failure. Part of this, she thought, was her own fault. He said he told her about the allergy long ago—why had she been so stupid to forget? Of course he would react that way. It *did* look suspicious. She could be better from now on, start getting things right. Their marriage did not have to end in tragedy.

She decided to stay, but vowed to never bake another pie.

Until now?

Chilled by the memory, she searches for a distraction—something to keep her mind off the thing on the windowsill—and sees the boiling water. At least there is that. And the bay leaf, the precious bay leaf, drifting so hopelessly among the tides. She wants to hold it, to caress it, to whisper soothingly that everything will be okay. There is thyme, too, pepper and paprika; the jar of salt sitting pretentiously away from the others, as if to say, *I contain iodide and you don't*.

It is important that she do something. She cannot simply stand there resenting the salt and daydreaming about the pie. If the recipe is lost forever, she must invent her own.

On the counter are four lemons: thick-skinned, ripe and wet as if recently washed. No lemons were washed today but her frazzled mind ignores this detail. She takes up a paring knife and confronts the citrus. She slices into the lemons with satisfying strokes. It feels good to be back on track, to be preparing things for a purpose. The fact that the lemons serve no purpose is not important. There will be something in the book that calls for lemons. If not, she can squeeze the juice onto lettuce and make a salad. Her husband hates salad, but not as much as he hates an empty table. They *will* serve a purpose. She will force them to.

Halfway through the third lemon, the blade slips. It slams hard, severing the thin web of flesh between her third and fourth finger. It is a hateful, bloodless cut that shrieks with pain as lemon juice pours into the gash. She jerks, startled by the sudden, acidic bite.

She washes her hands. The soap stings even worse than the initial cut. She grits her teeth and cries. She is hurt, of course, by the pain of the cut but more so by this additional failure. The lemons were a final attempt to improve an impossible situation and she has again shown herself incompetent.

She dries her hands on a paper towel and wraps it around the slit. She thinks about how many times she has been physically injured in this kitchen and wonders if the number is more or less than one thousand.

Behind her the boiling water bubbles over, plopping onto the hot stove with the hiss of snakes. She lowers the heat again and stirs. After a few circles the boil subdues.

With no other option she allows herself to be intrigued by the phantom pie. She turns to the curtains, watches them breathe with the breeze. A shadowy, circular object is visible atop the sill. Perhaps the pie is not an illusion after all. Perhaps she did make it herself, hours ago, while deep in thought. She might even risk serving it, just to see her husband's stunned expression before killing her. At least it would be one act of defiance.

She approaches the curtains cautiously. A sense of destiny propels her forward even as her body weakens with fear. The tell-tale silhouette reveals itself again—it could be a pie or a landmine. She lingers a limp finger toward the red curtains, draws back at the touch of rough fabric. The shadow protrudes and shapeshifts. Something appears to spike out of the center. Fragrance rushes forward: baked crust and blackberry filling. It is the definition of pleasant and yet she recognizes the odor as foreboding and reminiscent of death.

Abruptly, she rips apart the curtains and confronts the object.

She recognizes the pie instantly. It is, on all accounts, an exact replica of the one she prepared years before. The same pie that enraged her husband. It has the same flaws—crust too thin, slightly burnt—and the same perfections—thick, gooey consistency a midnight shade of purple. There is even the same dusting of powdered sugar on top, a last-minute idea which had been entirely her own and not mentioned in the book.

The single difference is that this pie has a thirteen inch kitchen knife stabbed directly into its center. She can see herself in the reflection of the blade.

She grasps the knife by the thick, black handle and tugs, slowly at first, like Arthur testing the sword in the stone. There is no surprise when it emerges with ease. A splatter of bluish goo slides off the tip as she wields it in the air.

The knife feels good in her hands, familiar. A sense of electricity sizzles around the room, around her. If she did prepare the pie in a blackened state of unawareness, perhaps she knew that she would encounter it now, in these desperate times, with this willingness to be empowered. Whatever message the pie is designed to send, she receives it in the most murderous way.

Tonight, she thinks, her husband will eat what she serves.

She picks up the pie and carries it to the dining table. Curls of steam rise from the hot filling as it cools. The smell is overwhelming, dizzying. She sets a single plate on a decorative doily at the head of the table. This is where her husband will sit—this is where he will die.

She stabs the knife into the pie again. Let it stay there for now. She has much to do before the clock strikes six.

First she must clean up the kitchen. If he sees the mess he will attack before she is prepared. There is no time to put everything back so she wheels an oversized trash can to the edge of the counter and sweeps assorted ingredients into it with one arm. Glass, plastic, cartons and other containers clang at the bottom. When all is done the can is nearly full. The empty kitchen brings a mixture of relief and depression, like casting off conspirators and finding herself completely alone.

All that remains is the recipe book, salt, lemons and pot of boiling water. With time running short, she has to plot the murder quickly. He will fight back, so she needs to finish him off fast—but it is also important that he suffer. No need to be tidy. The image of her cozy kitchen splattered with blood is a pleasant one.

The grandfather clock reads fifteen minutes to six.

She returns to the pie, pulls out the knife and rinses it off. She locates a sharpener and strokes the blade against ridged steel. The grinding, metallic noise is like music. There should be some symbolism to the massacre, she thinks. After all, this is not a freak killing. It is retrospective self-defense. He needs a taste of her daily routine. Some inkling of the misery she encounters in this kitchen.

A recipe occurs to her. "Salty Demise" she calls it and is surprised to find herself laughing at the idea. It is not the type of recipe that can be found in her book, but it should be. She decides to write it out on one of the blank pages:

Salty Demise
(Prep Time: Approx. 10-20 minutes)

1. Submerge knife in boiling water for 5-10 minutes, remove and pat dry
2. Soak blade in a marinade of lemon juice and soap
3. Sprinkle iodized salt onto blade
4. Serve hot

After scripting the recipe, she follows her directions to the letter. The salt sticks beautifully to the blade in the mix of lemon juice and soap. It sparkles in the artificial light, appearing decorative and whimsical, almost non-threatening. She likes that. A perfect deception.

It is six and the clock is striking. With the sound of each hour her confidence drains away. The knife almost drops from her hand as she props herself against the counter. The room feels as if it is swaying. Pain swirls through her arm, back and neck. It is only the memory of agony from long ago, she knows, but it feels crippling. What is she doing? What has gotten into her head? She is weak compared to him. He will laugh at her and beat her anyway. The knife will be slapped out of her hands like a toy and she will be helpless to retrieve it. Why did she have to make things worse?

As the sixth chime erupts throughout the house, she imagines that the walls are trembling, the pot rattling on the stove, dishes shattering. Cracks creeping from ceiling to floor, etching toward the kitchen where she stands. A cavern opens up, revealing the smoldering pit of hell. She can see herself falling into that pit, grasping uselessly for stray tree roots as she descends into darkness and heat.

Out of breath, steadying herself, she waits for the vision to pass. Her defiance, which seemed almost jovial earlier, has revealed its problems. She has been trained to fear this hour, how can she expect herself to misbehave? She is supposed to be scurrying about the kitchen, adding final garnishes and testing temperatures with tiny thermometers. She is not supposed to be plotting to kill her husband. It is like going against the course of nature. Would a clock experience this conflict if it chose to run backwards? Can she, thus designed, do anything but comply with normality?

The answers to these questions will soon reveal themselves, she thinks. It is 6:01 and there is the distinct noise of his car pulling into the gravel driveway. She hides the knife behind her back and retreats to the far corner of the kitchen to wait.

She does not have to wait long.

The front door creaks open on rusty hinges—he is inside. She can hear his distant, hoarse breath in the entryway. The closet opens, shuts. Heavy footsteps on the carpet—he is approaching the hallway already! Any moment he will be in the kitchen, he will see her and be suspicious. He will attack.

She stiffens her grip on the knife and flushes with new energy. She has not given up yet. Perhaps a conflict is exactly what she needs. A death match. A big bang—something so horrific it spins her life onto a new course. There can be a struggle, if that is what he wants. How it happens is not important, so long as it ends with her standing over his butchered body.

One stab is all it takes.

One stab is all it takes.

One stab is all it takes.

She repeats this like a mantra, exciting herself, allowing herself to boil. She is no longer the wooden spoon, she thinks. She hopes.

Suddenly, there he is. Framed in the hallway. Tall, thick, dressed in a collared shirt. His sleeves are rolled up to show off thin threads of arm muscle which have somehow remained from his adolescence. A receding head of dyed black hair is locked into place with some kind of lubricant. His face is the product of failed morning regimens: anti-wrinkle ointments, chemicals and pastes. The youthful charade is a poor performance, but she cannot deny that he remains attractive.

He is casual, unfurrowed and a little smug as he enters the kitchen with a newspaper under his arm. He probably made a good business deal today—if he is in the line of making business deals. She doesn't really know what he does. If he ever told her, it was probably a lie.

He does look like a business man, though. Or a politician, maybe. Someone who can break laws and get away with it by wearing a suit.

She can see now how he must have conned her. A small-town girl, painfully single and desperate for stability, pursued by an attractive older man. Three dates and they were engaged. Why stop and think? Everything was going so well. He met all her criteria—handsome and well-off. Her friends approved, her parents approved. They were, in fact, once a celebrated couple.

When did their celebrity end? After the first sign of abuse? After he broke her arm? It is difficult to remember life outside the kitchen. She recalls a decision to stop speaking with friends and family after the first black eye—they would only tell her to suffer through it and, worse, know her life was as miserable as before—but had she ceased communicating with them entirely? Unlikely. And yet she cannot think of an example to disprove this theory.

He enters the kitchen at a brisk pace and stops halfway to the dining room. His murky eyes whip round in her direction. He *is* suspicious, but not necessarily of her—he is staring at something beyond her. He sniffs the air curiously, animal-like. Trying to identify his dinner, she thinks. Will he smell the pie? How can he not?

She braces herself further against the wall, putting distance between them. At any moment, she thinks, he will rush forward with hands reaching out for her throat.

He does not move or alter his gaze, however. Something is off. He is anxious and perplexed, even looking a little scared. How long will it take for him to react? Should she say something? Try to soothe his nerves before he becomes enraged? Probably so, but what would she say? The thought of uttering another "Hello, darling" is unbearable.

Eventually he walks on, seats himself at the head of the table and unfolds the newspaper.

He's going to see the pie, she shrieks to herself. *Hurry—kill him now! Kill him before he sees!*

But, of course, she *wants* him to see the pie. That is part of the plan. He needs to know why this is happening and she needs to see recognition in those eyes before stabbing the blade between them.

He is reading something—a gossip article most likely—while she stands in the corner, holding her breath, preparing to end his life. How can he not sense the hatred in the room? The sweltering stench of blackberries and murder? It is all around her, swirling, pulsating; a hanging fog that creeps just below the throat. What does he think is going on? That she is standing there, frantic and frozen, to allow him time to settle in? Is he waiting for her to serve iced tea and pot roast?

She is about to act when he turns in his seat. A corner of newspaper folds down, allowing him to squint in her direction. He looks puzzled again, as if noticing a tiny speck on the carpet and debating whether it is a stain or lint fuzz.

She cannot stand it any longer. Whether he sees the pie or not, he must die. If she is going to do it, she has to do it now.

The knife comes out, salty, lemon-soaked and still hot. She raises it in the air and lunges at him. She shuts her eyes tight to avoid seeing the bloody act. She is afraid witnessing it will cause her to stop. When all is done she can observe every drop of gore, but not until then.

Her attack is on target. The knife swings down and penetrates flesh. She can feel the blade ooze through tendons and hit bone. She rips it out and brings it down again, harder, faster. More soft flesh. Again—she hits something hard. His skull? No time to ponder, she arches back and takes another slice, throwing all of her emotion into it, all of her anger. He must be dead by now, but she cannot stop. There is still too much he has to pay for. She swings again—the handle is slick with blood. She tightens her grip. Again—

Slower now, her strength wavering, she is on rhythm with the clock.

As the pendulum sways, the blade rises and falls again.

Again. Again. Again.

Again.

Exhausted, her body goes limp and falls to the floor. The knife clatters on the tile nearby. Her eyes are still closed and soaked with tears. They are tears of sadness, happiness, anger and redemption. A weight has been lifted, a sentence pardoned. She is free.

"OH, GOD!"

It is a man's voice. *His* voice, agonized but still very much alive.

Her eyes snap open. She is on the floor, the knife nearby, but the dining room is immaculate white. No blood. No slaughtered body. Her husband is still seated at the table, entirely unharmed, massaging his temples. The newspaper has been discarded, at least, and he appears to be distressed about something.

"WILL IT EVER STOP?" he screams, pounding a fist against the table. There is not a scratch on his body. How is this possible? "I've repented," he continues, whispering now. "I've changed."

Tears leak down his face. He cups his forehead in his palm. "I went too far. It was a terrible, evil thing. But I'm sorry. I'M SORRY!" he yells the final apology to the room and slumps into the chair. It is clear that he is tormented, but by what? The knife has failed. He is still alive.

She crawls to her knees, picks up the knife and inches toward his thigh beneath the table. With a quick plunge, she stabs it into his leg. She can feel the exquisite sensation of metal piercing skin, muscle and ligaments ripping, but the blade itself vanishes into a mist when it touches him. No blood, only vapor. Still, he winces in reaction.

"Get out of my head!" he howls, crying fully now. Into his hands. Blubbery and pathetic.

The grandfather clock drones on. There is an uncanny feeling of déjà vu and sense that her time is running out. She stabs his leg one more time. He yells again, not hurt physically but mentally.

"Please," he whimpers, almost inaudible. "Please—stop."

A haze settles over the room. It is as if she is watching the scene from afar. He is still sobbing in the chair and she is somehow floating away. She can feel her mind start to loosen, to tire. Images blur, leaving only vague traces of grey and black streaks. The incessant ticking of the clock amplifies, reverberates. Time feels ambiguous. Do the ticking noises represent seconds or minutes, hours or days?

There is so much mist. Her body seems to be part of it, mixing with the moisture, evaporating. Unconsciousness is everywhere.

When her mind returns it is another day, another loop. She is standing in the kitchen, preparing a new recipe from an old book. How curious, she thinks, that there is already a pot of water boiling on the stove. She must have prepared it earlier and forgot.

And where did that pie come from? What does it mean?

No time to worry. There is much to do before the clock strikes six.

("Before the Clock Strikes Six" was previously published by author on Amazon.com)

A Nice Guy

By R.B. Roth

David was a regular guy. He was of average height; he wore his hair in the same style as any other middle class American college student; his wardrobe alternated between khakis, jeans, and cargo shorts; and he ran 5Ks despite his obvious lack of a six pack. He did not stand out in any way, but he had one advantage over everyone else like him: he was a real nice guy.

David went to college to study accounting. He figured that it would be a respectable, steady job with a decent income. He went to a small, Jesuit university outside of his hometown of Cleveland, since his parents said that they would only pay his tuition if he went to a Catholic college. Having heard so many horror stories about local kids who had graduated with crippling debt, he agreed to this arrangement.

It was at the start of his second semester, on the first day of his introduction to psychology class, that he saw her. She entered the classroom with her backpack slung over one shoulder. She wore a cropped sweater and a pair of old jeans that somehow both concealed and accentuated her figure. Her hair fell down her back like spun sunshine. Her expression sparkled. David could not take his eyes off of her.

She took the seat in front of him, as if she felt just as drawn to him. He smiled to himself. It must be destiny.

He discovered that her name was Emma, and that she was a year older than him. David did not mind this – in fact, he found the idea of dating an older woman intriguing. He spent the first few weeks staring at her hair and resisting the urge to touch it, imagining the day when it would be his right. Before the first exam, David gathered his courage and suggested that they study together. He was thrilled when she agreed.

The night before the test, David walked to Emma's dorm building, which was on the other side of campus. She buzzed him in. David climbed the stairs to the second floor and knocked on her door. Some boy answered. David vaguely recognized him from class.

"Hey," the boy said with minimal interest.

David grunted in reply. He looked past him and saw Emma spraying a girl with perfume.

"Marilyn Monroe wore Chanel No. 5," Emma was saying. "It just smells so incredible!" She then noticed David. "Great, you're here!"

"Yeah," David mumbled as he glared at the greasy-faced boy.

"Did you meet Evan and Angie? They're in our class, too." She nudged Angie's arm and grinned. "They're in lurvvvvveeee." she sang.

A wave of relief enveloped David as he watched Angie blush. Out of the corner of his eye he saw that Evan also looked embarrassed. David grinned as everyone sat on the floor in a circle and pulled out their study supplies. Evan seemed like a cool guy, he thought. Maybe the four of them could double date sometime.

* * *

All his life David heard the story of how his parents came to be a couple. He hung on every word, craving new details that would fill in the road map that he was constructing in his mind.

"I fell in love with her the moment I saw her," his father explained. "She was so beautiful. I thought her hair was brighter than the sun. But the timing was wrong. She was dating someone else. So we were just friends. We had to be. We had too many common interests to not be friends. As far as I was concerned, once I found out she was unavailable, she was just one of the guys. I didn't just sit there waiting for her to come around."

"No, you had plenty of girlfriends," his mother agreed with a playful lilt in her voice.

His father smiled. He placed his hands on his hips with pride. "How could anyone say no to all of this?" He asked as he barreled his chest.

His mother giggled. "I did."

"You eventually came to your senses," he teased with affection. He turned to David and explained, "She had to grow out of her bad boy phase before she could appreciate a nice guy like me."

"You had your own phase at that time, too," his mother laughed, watching him with tenderness from underneath her eyeglasses.

His father made an exaggerated show of staring off in the distance. "Ah! Caroline Malinsky! What a body!" He reached out his hands as if he could trace the memory.

David's mother chuckled as she smacked her husband's arm with the back of her hand. "Oh, you behave! Do you want me to tell David about Bobby Wells?" She turned her gaze to her son. "Bobby was 6'4" and had these beautiful brown curls and the most piercing blue eyes. I was so in love with him." She giggled in nostalgia.

"You looked ridiculous standing next to Bobby." David's father laughed. He side-hugged his very petite wife. "But you look perfect standing next to me." He kissed her cheek. Each retelling of their love story ended with a kiss on the cheek.

So when David found out that Emma was an English major, he became one as well. It doubled his workload and he had to put up with pretentious poetry, but it meant they could have some common interests. Just like his parents.

* * *

Emma kissed David once.

She had just broken up with another one of her pretty-boy frat bros when she stopped by his dorm room so that they could exchange and discuss each other's research papers. When David opened the door he noticed her red, glistening eyes.

"Emma, what's wrong?" he asked, his voice full of concern.

She entered his room as she shrugged. "Nothing," she replied. "Everything. I don't know." She started to cry.

David placed his arm around her shoulders. He breathed in her hair. The scent made his lungs feel warm. "Tell me what happened," he said.

Emma hunched over as if she was an actress in a melodrama. "*Brad* happened," she moaned. "He texts me in the middle of the night all the time, begging me to come over, but when I asked him just one time for a ride to the library he says he's too busy. And then he keeps bugging me for sexy pics. I mean, I don't want to end up on one of those revenge porn sites. So I tell him no, and that's when he calls me the 'anti-boner', like that's even a thing. I told him to just lose my number and never text me again."

"Emma, he doesn't sound like a nice guy. He doesn't deserve you."

"He's *not* a nice guy," she agreed. She sniffed and looked embarrassed. "The stupid thing is I still like him." She rested her head on David's shoulder. "I'm just so tired of being used."

"I would never use you," he whispered, staring at his fidgeting fingers.

"I know," she said. She lifted his chin and looked into his eyes. He wanted to kiss her, but he hesitated. She did not. It only lasted a moment, but to David it was an exquisite lifetime.

Until she said, "I wish more guys were like you."

David recoiled from the verbal stabbing. Emma did not notice. She sat on his bed and declared, "I think I just need a break, you know? Focus on school and stuff."

David nodded. "Maybe that's a good idea," he agreed. His voice was hollow. He was disappointed that it meant that he would have to wait longer for his reward, but at least no one else would take her away.

"I'm not ready for a relationship," she continued. "I need to find out who I am or something. I'm just gonna study and have fun with my friends."

David smiled. "Like me!" he said with more enthusiasm than he felt.

Emma grinned as she mussed his hair. "Exactly!"

* * *

"The important thing was I didn't sit around waiting for her," David's father told him when he was visiting home one weekend. "I dated other girls; I set goals for myself and worked towards them; I built myself a life. That way, when your mother finally came back I had something to offer her." He paused to take a swig of his craft beer. "I had a good job and my own life. If I did nothing but pine over her then she would have saw me as nothing more than a pathetic loser. And she would have been right. No woman wants a doormat. She wants someone strong, who knows when to take charge, but who also respects her."

His mother nodded. "It's true. I wouldn't have given him a chance if all he did was write me love poetry all day." She chuckled. "Love poems are great and all, but I would have thought he was weird if he spent so much time thinking about me – especially when I wasn't thinking of him."

"Oh, you weren't, huh?" his father asked with a twinkle in his eye. "The truth comes out after all these years."

His mother laughed. "You loved the challenge; admit it."

His father nodded. "It's true." He turned to face David. "*Romeo and Juliet* isn't magic. It isn't romance. It's a couple of kids making up fantasies about each other. Real love takes patience and timing and work. And it doesn't make you want to kill yourself or anyone else once you find it."

* * *

"David, I just want to make sure that everything's ok with us."

David was walking to class when Emma ran up behind him. He stopped and turned to face her. "Why wouldn't things be ok?" he asked. He watched her lips as she spoke. How he wanted to feel those lips again!

Emma blushed despite the early winter wind. "Because... you know... because of that kiss."

David smiled. "I liked that kiss," he admitted.

To his surprise, Emma did not return his smile. "Yes, it was really nice, and you were so sweet not to make a big deal about it. You must have tasted all the alcohol on my breath."

David hadn't noticed any alcohol. Nor did she seem drunk. He nodded anyway.

"I've been screwing up so much lately. I just don't want to screw up our friendship."

She paused. David felt another opportunity to make a move. But he could not tell if she wanted it. He took her limp hand in his and regarded her with reassurance. "Nothing could screw up our friendship," he said, despite how he felt. "It can only get better."

Emma blushed again. She looked uncomfortable. David dropped her hand.

Emma brushed her hair from her face. Her sunshine hair. She took a deep breath and smiled. "Good. I'm glad you said that. Because I meant it when I said that I'm taking a break from boys. I don't want to date anyone right now."

By the end of the week, Emma had accepted Brad's apology, and they were a couple again.

* * *

When she graduated college, Emma decided to backpack around Southeast Asia. David wished that he could go with her, but he still had another year of school. He reminded himself that once he had a degree and a good job, he would have something real to offer the girl of his dreams.

David dated others while Emma was away, but they did not mean anything to him. He told himself that they were just time-fillers. Practice. It was the same formula his father followed before the time was right to woo his mother. But as soon as one of the girls started talking about the future he moved on. None of them could compare to Emma. None of them understood him. None of them *got* him. Not like Emma.

He followed her on all of the social media sites, although she only occasionally posted updates and photos. David tried to keep in touch by sending her private messages. She initially responded, but she soon stopped answering altogether. His heart cringed at the fear that he was losing her, but then he remembered his parents. They had to grow apart before they inevitably grew together. So David waited. He fed his patience by studying her account every day. Each of her infrequent posts made him feel closer to her. Whenever she posted photos of any guys, he monitored their accounts, too, until he found evidence that they had moved on without Emma.

When he finished his degree he got a job with an impressive starting salary at a suburban accounting firm outside of Cleveland. As he lived with his parents, he was able to save the bulk of his income. After a year he bought a small Cape Cod that bordered the Metroparks. It was the perfect starter house.

Almost two years to the day since David last saw Emma, she posted that she missed her hometown and was moving back to Cleveland to get her MFA at their old university. David could not believe his eyes when he read her post during his lunch break at work. He wanted to cheer, to jump on a couch, to cry... but he refrained since such things were not done at the accounting firm. Instead he planned how he could get back in touch with her. He rejected the idea of simply emailing her. Their entwined fates demanded something much less pedestrian than an easily forgotten email. Besides, he didn't want her to think he was a pathetic loser who had been pining for her since the day she left. He was more than that. He was her destiny.

Over the next few months, diligent Google and social media research allowed David to discover the general area to which Emma had moved. He started spending every weekend in her neighborhood, hoping to run into her. He focused on the coffee shops, since she had often bragged about her coffee addiction. He drank coffee from open to close in a different place each weekend. He brought his laptop so that he could pretend to be some poser working on a novel, when really he was playing online games or reading newspapers from around the world. After several weeks of this, David was starting to get discouraged and a little bored, but he kept at it.

After some time, his perseverance paid off. He glanced up from his game to see Emma standing in line. She looked like she had just come from the gym. Her much shortened hair was pulled back and sweaty, but it still shone brighter than the sun. She had lost a little weight, but to David she never looked more soft and feminine. He inhaled deeply to calm his nerves and approached her.

"Emma?" he said, as if he was uncertain.

Her eyes grew wide with delight when she saw David. "Oh, my God! David! I can't believe it!" she squealed. She pulled him in for a hug.

David pressed his face against her so he could taste her sweat. He did not move until Emma broke the hug and stepped back. "I'm sorry. I shouldn't have hugged you like that. I just got out of my spin class. I must really stink."

David smiled. "Not at all. Don't worry about it." He paused, wondering if it would be weird to go in for another hug.

"So how are you?" Emma asked as she picked up her coffee. "Tell me everything."

David invited her to sit down with him. He told her about his job and his house, and then she briefly outlined the high points of her travels. David grinned and nodded as if he listened, unable to hear any other sound but Emma's voice. This moment was worth everything. It was the moment when his prize became within his reach.

After about 10 minutes, Emma looked at the time and announced that she had to go. David's heart fell, but he kept his face cheerful. "Maybe we can meet for lunch sometime for a *real* catch-up," he suggested.

"Uh, yeah, that would be great," Emma said.

"Maybe Wednesday? My treat."

Emma laughed. "No grad student can turn down free food. I'll meet you here at noon." She waved her fingers and started for the door. "See ya!"

David waved back. Once she was out of sight he sat down and dedicated a moment to relive their meet-cute.

As he packed up his laptop, he realized that he did not ask for her number; nor did she ask for his.

* * *

On Wednesday, David waited in the coffee shop, barely able to breathe. He was afraid that Emma wouldn't show or, worse, he would freeze and be unable to participate in an entertaining conversation. He kept watching the door, feeling more and more like a loser with each glance. Finally, he saw her approach the coffee shop, and he exhaled. Emma could have blown him off, but she didn't. Because on some level she knew that she was his.

He stood to greet her. She approached him with her arms wide. They hugged. She smelled just like her dorm room the first night they studied together. Chanel No. 5.

"I am so glad that I ran into you." she exclaimed. "I meant to email you, but who uses email anymore, right? Anyway, I've been so busy moving back here and starting school and stuff. Did you know I'm back at school?"

David nodded. "You mentioned that on your page, right?"

"Oh, yeah," she said. "I guess I could have messaged you over that. I haven't been on it much lately."

"Really?" He said, as if he hadn't noticed. *Play it cool.* He breathed.

Emma giggled. "No one really uses those things much anymore. I mean, old people do when they have babies and stuff, right? Although I guess I could post pictures of my cat. Did I tell you I adopted a cat?"

David giggled with her. He was so happy to be with her again, laughing like they always did. Emma understood him. Their connection was beyond physical.

"Anyway, so much has happened since I graduated. Asia was so amazing. You have to go to Thailand and do the full moon festival."

"The full moon festival?"

Emma nodded. "Hang on. Let me get a coffee, and I'll tell you everything."

"If I remember correctly, what you drink can hardly be called coffee."

Emma laughed. "Shut up! There's coffee in it."

David watched her as she walked towards the counter to place her order. Emma was just as he remembered her. Her hair still glistened; her laughter still strong and infectious; mischief still sparkled in her eyes. None of the other girls that David knew had the life in them that Emma had. Emma had never needed constant reassurance from him or anyone. Emma knew who she was, and she never held back her enthusiasm. She made David feel warm and accepted.

When Emma returned to their table, she told David about her travels in greater detail. She described the hostels and how friendly everyone was. She recounted hiking in Chiang Mai, the temples of Ankgor Wat, and the beaches of Viet Nam. David listened to every word, for what better way to admire her than to let her see him listening?

"What about your classes?" David asked. "Does the old alma mater seem different now that you've seen the world?"

Emma snickered. "It's exactly the same," Emma replied. "Although they are building an extension to the science building." She reached out and punched his arm with affection. The same way his mother teased his father. "What about you? Any girlfriends you want to tell me about?"

Is she jealous? "Well..." he blushed.

Emma's mouth fell open in excitement. "There *is* someone, isn't there?"

"I don't know," he mumbled as he stared into his coffee. *Should he say something?*

"Oh, my God! Who is it?"

David shook his head. Now is not the time. "No one! I mean, I'm just seeing how things go."

Emma smiled. "That's smart. That's what I'm doing."

David raised his eyes from his coffee as his heart paused. "What?"

Emma blushed. "There's this guy in my poetry class. He is so sweet. You'd be so proud of me. He's nothing like the guys I dated in college."

"Uh, what do you mean?" he asked through his dry throat.

"Well, he's bald for one thing. But he shaves his head, so it's still cool."

"Uh, yeah."

"He is such a good writer. He's been published and everything. And he taught himself to play the guitar. He is so creative."

David flattened his lips and nodded.

"I don't think I've ever met anyone with whom I've had so much in common." Emma giggled. "Did you hear that? *With whom!*"

"Are you in love with him?"

"I don't know. I only just met him. But I really think that he might be the one. Maybe." She lowered her eyes and tried to suppress her excitement. "I don't know."

David took a sip of his coffee and felt his heart drown. He hesitated before he spoke. "Uh, he sounds kind of pretentious," he mumbled.

Emma's smile disappeared in shock. "What?"

David's frustration and Emma's surprise fueled his courage. "He sounds just like all the jerks you dated in college. He's just going to hurt you." He cleared his throat. "Whatever."

Emma flushed. "You don't even know him. He's nothing like those guys." She stood up and grabbed her purse. "If I didn't know better, I'd say you're acting jealous."

"I just think you're making a mistake. And I hate watching you make mistakes." *Please stay*, he wanted to scream.

"Shut up! I don't care what you think. It's my life. I'll date who I want."

"Emma..."

"I can't believe I thought you were a nice guy." She turned and moved to the door.

"I am a nice guy!" David yelled and his fist hammered the table. The entire coffee shop went silent. David grabbed his jacket and raced out the door just in time to see Emma turn a corner. He followed her as she ran home, until he found out where she lived. In college David thought that Emma needed protection from all the guys. Now he realized that what she really needed was protection from herself. David was there for her, more than anyone else ever could be. Always.

* * *

When David was in high school, he asked his father for advice about how to approach his crush.

"Just be her friend," his father advised. "The best romances start out as friendships. Look at your mom and me. If she had gone out with me when we first met, we probably wouldn't be together today. Neither of us knew what we wanted then. But we became friends instead and really got to know each other. Then, when we were both ready, I told her how I felt."

"But what if she doesn't like me back?"

"Then you move on."

His mother, who had been listening from the other room, stuck her head around the door. "How could anyone not like you back?" she asked. "You're so sweet and nice, and you're just as handsome as your father."

"Mommm..."

"I'm serious!" she said as she entered the room. She tousled David's hair. "Whoever you choose is going to be so lucky."

* * *

David was waiting in his car in the parking lot outside of Emma's apartment building. He had been waiting ever since he watched Emma and her poet leave for their date. He considered following them but decided against it. After all, it's not like he was a stalker.

At a little before midnight, a car pulled into the parking lot and stopped in front of the door to Emma's building. David's heart deflated as he watched Emma invite her date inside. He did not understand. Emma had such a fun lunch with David, regardless of how it ended. He had listened to all her stories and laughed at the appropriate moments and complimented her life decisions, and she repaid him by once again falling for another poser bad boy with an acoustic guitar.

He wanted to give Emma everything, and she just refused to accept it.

David sat in his car, staring at the front door. And sat. And sat. He would not leave until that tattooed meathead walked out of the building. He did not notice the passage of time; he was too angry. David had put in enough time. He had been Emma's friend. He had never pressured her. He was a *nice guy*. He deserved to be recognized for that. He deserved her love.

After a couple of hours, he saw the door to the apartment building open. He watched Emma's date exit and walk towards his car. Seeing this man drive away did not abate David's fury. He was tired of the way Emma had treated him. He was tired of being overlooked.

David got out of his car and moved to the building with purpose. He pressed the intercom button.

After a few seconds she answered. "Hello?" Her voice sounded uncertain.

"It's David. From college."

"David? Why are you here? It's like two in the morning."

"I need to talk to you. It's urgent."

After a pause, she buzzed him in. David climbed the stairs to the second floor and knocked on her door.

Emma answered. Her polite smile faded when she saw his fury. David noticed, and that made him even angrier.

"David, what are you doing here?" Emma asked. Her voice trembled. "How did you know where I live?" Her orange tabby stood at her feet, hissing.

David pushed past Emma and entered her apartment. Emma hesitated before she closed the door behind him. "David, are you ok?"

David's teeth clenched as he seethed, "Did you have a good time?"

"What?"

"Did. You. Have. A. Good. Time."

Emma furrowed her brow. "With Tim?"

"Yes, with *fucking* Tim."

Emma flushed with discomfort. "David, I don't think that's any of your business."

"Of course it's my business!" David yelled. "You're my business! What do I have to do to make you understand? I've supported you, I've been your friend, I comforted you every time another one of these jerks hurt you…"

"And I really appreciate that…"

David cut her off. "Shut up! You don't appreciate anything! You treat me like shit, like I'm some sort of pet dog. I'm not a dog; I'm a man! And I have so much to give you. Why can't you see that?"

Emma stepped back, inching towards the decorative fireplace. She eyed the marble mantel on which she had placed her keys. She kept her pepper spray on the keychain.

"I have been nothing but loyal to you since the day I met you. Why can't you get it into your head that we belong together? That I would treat you like a queen?" David paused to wipe a tear from his eye. He

91

stared at his finger, as if he was surprised to see the moisture. "Don't you remember how you kissed me? Didn't that mean anything to you?"

Emma's eyes reflected the sympathy she suddenly felt for him. She reached out to touch his arm. "David, I'm sorry you're hurting, but I just don't feel that way about you," she said in a soft voice. She felt his arm stiffen, but she continued. "I just think we work best as friends."

David's breath grew heavier, more rapid. He looked away from his hand and back to Emma, his stare becoming harder and more incredulous. By the time their eyes met, his were flashing a fiery, hateful glare.

"How would you know?" he bellowed. Emma released his arm. She ran to the fireplace. David followed her, walking as if he had grown a foot in height. "How would you fucking know?"

She grabbed the keys and tried to point the pepper spray at David, but her fingers were stiff with fear. She dropped the keys. She stooped to retrieve them, but she never had a second chance to take aim. Before she was able to stand erect, David's arm smashed across her face. The force knocked her against the mantel. When her chin hit the marble, her neck snapped at an unnatural angle. She fell to the ground.

David watched with horror. He collapsed onto his knees and wrapped his arms around her. "Emma?" he cried. "Emma, please, no, wake up. Wake up! Please! I'm sorry. I'm so sorry! It was an accident!" He rubbed his tear-stained face in her hair – her golden sunshine, her vibrant life. "Please!" His voice was muffled.

After a few minutes of despair, of burying his tears into her flesh, David sat up. He brushed the hair from her face as he sniffed. He took a labored breath and forced a smile. "You're gonna be ok," he promised, finding peace in his words. "I'll take care of you. You'll be ok."

He gathered her into his arms, holding her like he had always dreamed. Her body was limp. He picked her up to take her to his car, leaving the door to her apartment open as he left. The orange cat followed him into the hall, emitting a plaintive meow.

The night was dead. None but the hall lights shone from Emma's apartment complex. The only sounds were of crickets and his footsteps. He laid her in the back seat of his car and regarded her with affection.

He then drove her to his house.

* * *

It had been a long day at work, and David was relieved to get home. He dropped his leather messenger bag on the side table, opened it, and pulled out a smaller bag from the department store. He walked upstairs, passed his tiny bedroom, and went to the much larger guest room. The door was closed. He knocked.

Without waiting for a response, he opened the door and entered. "Hey! How was your day?" he asked. No answer. "Work was such a pain today," he continued. "It was practically non-stop. But I did manage to sneak away and get you a present." He sat on the edge of the bed and opened the bag. "It's perfume. Chanel No. 5. I remember seeing it in your old dorm room. Remember? *That* was a long time ago." He laughed and unwrapped the perfume. He sprayed some above the bed. "Well I guess that smells a little better," he said and then added in haste, "Oh, don't worry. I know it's not your fault. I'll figure something out. But the perfume helps, right?" He rose from the bed and crossed the room to adjust the thermostat on the industrial-strength air conditioner that he had bought. He chuckled to himself. "Pretty soon I'll be able to see my own breath in here."

He looked back towards the bed and gazed upon his one true love. He still could not believe that after so much time and patience, she was his. Warmth flushed over his body, despite the refrigerated temperatures. He smiled. "I really love you, Emma," he said. "I told you I would take care of you."

He returned to her bedside and sat beside her, their hips touching. He stroked her hair with his hand, trying to bring out the spun sunshine that had dulled since she had moved in to his house. His fingers caught on a tiny knot, causing a chunk of scalp to come off in his grasp.

"Oh! Sorry, Emma!" David said. He pressed the loose scalp against her head. "I'll get something to fix that. Tomorrow." He gazed at her and added, "You are still the most beautiful woman I have ever seen." He leaned over and touched her dry lips to his. "I will never leave you," he whispered.

David stayed with her for a few more minutes before he went downstairs to make dinner, taking with him the untouched plate he brought up for Emma the night before. He closed the door behind him so that the cold would not escape. All of her dinners had gone uneaten, but he wanted to provide for her, so he continued to make them. He placed a pot of water on the stove to boil. While he waited he opened a can of cat food. The orange tabby rubbed David's legs in anticipation. David scoffed at it.

"You're just pretending to like me so I'll give you this food," he said. The cat meowed. "You can act like you like me all you want, but that doesn't mean I'll ever love you. You're not entitled to this food or anything else. I only went back for you because of Emma, and you never even go upstairs to visit her." He set the bowl on the floor. "Stupid cat," he muttered.

As far as David could tell, the cat spent most of its' time in the basement and only came up to the kitchen for meals. David did not care. The cat made Emma happy, and David's whole life was for Emma. As long as he had her, he did not need anything else.

Wednesday's Child

By Jon Michael Kelley

"Good morning, Miss M."

The voice, lecherous as a dank cellar draft, seemed to travel low to the ground, as if slithering out from beneath a rock. She instantly froze, the spoon halfway to her mouth. She'd heard that voice once before, here on this very same glade, and knew that it originated from a primal and universally shared nightmare. Her skin, pupils, every follicle of hair reacted protectively as icy adrenaline surged to oil her limbs. She dared not turn around, as she knew with all certainty that what had crept upon her was a lethal, liquid-black grotesquery unparalleled in her world.

Highly venomous, but not a snake. Not any reptile.

"Sorry to interrupt your breakfast," said the Spider, "but I've again intentions to make you my own."

* * *

Greta Muffet turned the handle and unleashed the flatulence of ancient plumbing. The sink and surrounding counter bucked and hiccupped as the spigot coughed up air and spittle like an emphysemic before finally releasing a meager stream of rust-tinted water.

Eventually colors and pressures equalized, but not without some grumblings. *Much like the inner pipes of an old man*, she thought, although it was an old woman for whom she made this thrice-weekly trip; her dedication to the tired, to the infirm.

Or, to be quite accurate, the convalescent.

She placed the kettle beneath the flow, and waited patiently. It was tea time, a particularly endearing staple of her country, just as was the morality angle, although she normally didn't have *her* tea until five, when she preferred fancier flavors from the Darjeeling regions over those with names of once-popular Prime Ministers. But Lilith Dodd was an old woman and was stubbornly fond of her Earl Grey at noon. Fond the same way she once was of her many children, all grown and long gone now. Gone for good, the grudges of incessant whippings and diets of thin broth keeping them away.

As mentioned, Lilith Dodd is an old woman and now lives a mostly solitary life, one grown sedentary inside a largely dilapidated, laceless shoe, held together only by prayer, and of course the cobbler's annual stitching efforts. It stunk vaguely of mink oil and spilt wine, and its many curtains when sent fluttering in distant rooms suggested a lively haunting by a troupe of barefoot children.

Greta winced. Through the kitchen window, the late afternoon sun was at just the right angle to be making an effervescent spectacle of the old woman's porcelain egg collection from the adjacent dining room. All examples were neatly arranged upon tiny stands behind the curved glass of an old oak hutch. Some bore intricate carvings, some were gilded, others hinged and painted with opulent designs... Greta took almost as much pleasure in them as did Lilith, the faux Fabergé ones especially.

Greta Muffet lifted the kettle from the sink and onto an adjacent gas burner, one of three belonging to a necessarily thin though free-standing porcelain stove of a previous century's design.

"A pinch of orange rind, a teaspoon of honey," Lilith mulishly reminded from her rocker, creaking away, "then a quick stir or two to keep the color sunny."

Greta smiled, just a little. "I've not forgotten, Aunt Lily." Not a true aunt, but after so long it got to feeling that way, so certain affectations found purchase, and stuck.

"And I should think a halfpenny roll would be in proper order, dear."

"No rolls, I'm afraid, nor crumpets," Greta said, "but I can have you a vanilla scone in a jiff."

"Warmed with clotted cream, then."

"Of course."

She adjusted the flame, then her shawl (always a nagging draft here in the shoe), and stared out the window above the sink; beyond the tilted plane of a flower planter and the golden heads of its drooping mums; beyond the bleached designs and leaking limbs of long-discarded toys and into a starkness that, daytime or night, always seemed to saturate in any direction the unenthusiastic distance of her sight.

She brought her focus back in; back to the four partitioned panes (*spring, summer, fall and winter*, she mused), and found that they were edged with grime and mildew; so much like the cataracts of regret that have built upon the periphery of her own seasons; upon the lens of her reminiscence. She reached out and lightly fingered the hazing, her first impression to liken it to a thin layer of webbing, of spun silk - but she quickly jerked away from that comparison despite its aptness. Not to do so was to invite a profound depressive mood.

Or, to be quite accurate, agitate an already existing one.

She sighed. *Wednesday's child is full of woe.*

Lilith did the best she could to stretch out her left leg, giving acute consideration to the seeping bandages thick around her calf. "Doctor Salinas mentioned that the wound's healing nicely," she said, "and the scarring should be minimal, but a dent it will undoubtedly leave." *...creak, creak, creak...* "Just an awful, awful bite. What was it that he called it? 'Necrotic' something..."

"Necrotic arachnidism," Greta said, specific with the consonants.

"Yes, yes, a most defiling tongue-twister." Lilith shivered. "The punctures are abhorrent, their smell growing sour, one can't possibly take a long-enough shower."

Greta agreed, having once experienced the leprous feelings that were the aftereffect of her own encounter. The second one. And although she'd not been bitten as had Lilith, she often wished otherwise. "By the way, how are you doing with the antibiotics?" she asked. "They still making you nauseous?"

"I'm making sure to take them with bread and dairy," Lilith said. "Oh, did I tell you that the president of the homeowners association came by yesterday? Apparently, he wants me to speak at the next meeting. As ruthless crimes go, mine has been considered brutal enough to hopefully inspire a majority vote on the implementation of a Neighborhood Watch program." *...creak... creak...creak...* "I'm thinking of showing, but I've no way of going."

Still staring vacantly at the window, Greta said, "I'll be happy to take you. Just give me some notice."

"Then notice you shall have. Next Tuesday at eight pm sharp. Wee Willie Winkie's place."

Greta simply nodded, then opened a faded tin and began spooning its dark contents into a tea ball.

The creaking chair stopped. "You seem especially distant today, dear," Lilith observed. "To mention Wee Willie reminds me that you both wear enduring garments, his made of night clothes, yours of melancholy." The chair started up again. "What has you so occupied?"

Greta finally turned, her fingers fumbling at the embroidered fringe of her apron. "It's just ... it's just that we almost lost you. If I had acted responsibly, unselfishly, those many years ago... Well, I like to think that the vicious assault upon you would have never happened, as the Spider would still be incarcerated. Perhaps even dead by now, a victim of his own irony with the isolation having ultimately left him a dry, hollow shell."

The kettle began to whistle. Greta snatched it and immediately poured the boiling water into a cup for such intentions; beneath was a matching saucer, both designs of twisting vines.

"You did what you had to do, dear," Lilith said. "No one knows how they will act when confronted with the Spider."

"That's because no one has lived to tell after being bitten," Greta said, fondly steeping the tea ball. "Except you."

Lilith shrugged diffidently. "What's most important is that you forgive yourself. It's been too many years to carry that guilt."

As if there should be a statute of limitations for that kind of remorse, Greta thought.

* * *

A black, keratin dagger caressed her cheek. "Sweet, sweet Miss. M. Soon, we shall see." His breath was fusty, slightly fetid, and she turned away. There, she beheld the bulbous abdomen as it moved in liquid, vulgar ways. Two black spinnerets groped the air like the fleshy stubs of an amputee, then a fine spray of silk lighted upon her shoes. "Just in case you were to find your heels again," said the Spider.

Greta pinched her eyes closed, and begged wetly from a trembling lip. She said that there were things she wished to live for; that youth had all but abandoned her, this was true, but life still maintained a certain preciousness, and was not desired to be lost just yet. Not like this.

Dear, sir, please: not like this.

"Perhaps an exchange, then?" *offered the Spider.*

"An exchange?"

Another black appendage wrapped around her waist and pulled her closer, her tuffet no longer holding her weight. "A covenant, if you will. A solemn agreement just between us."

Her knees gave out, yet she still remained upright in the Spider's hydraulic grasp. She was still in possession of her bowl, though it was sloping now, her curds and whey slipping out, warm on her fingers as were the tears upon her cheeks.

"The three little kittens, all plump with pie," *whispered the Spider.* "Tell me their whereabouts when their mother is indisposed, and I shall leave you to only the silk around your ankles. If not, then I will leave your desiccated remains to the discretion of the wind."

* * *

Greta sighed. "I didn't make a clean getaway," she reminded. "For my own freedom I told him when and where the three kittens could be found unprotected. I practically drew him a map!"

"Yes, it was you, or the fur balls," she agreed. "Difficult choices. But it's not like you betrayed your own kind. You followed a hierarchy. You know your link in the food chain. Nothing to be ashamed of. Besides, if it had been me, I would have sold out Little Tom Tinker's dog. Keeps crapping in my begonias." She cackled at this, then resumed with a shake of her finger: "You can bet your pease porridge that had the roles been reversed and those kitties had had larger brains and opposable thumbs, then you'd have been offered up just as effortlessly had directions to your own whereabouts been solicited."

Just as effortlessly? Aghast, Greta said, "I assure you that my decision was not without a fair amount of angst! And if I may remind you, their mother had to be put down, the grief having left her without a proper mind."

"I didn't mean to minimize the consequences, dear, just illuminate the obvious."

Greta shook her head. "Why I couldn't muster the nerve to run the second time…"

"Your decision not to will haunt you till the end," Lilith guaranteed her. Then, with less fuss than one might have expected, she stood, wavering ever so slightly. She cinched her frazzled terry robe, and said, "Let's forget the scone. I'll just take my tea in the living room."

"On the couch, then," Greta said after her. "I'll fix you up with some fresh dressings, and iodine."

Lilith ignored the couch and sought the comfort of another chair; this one encompassing with frayed wingbacks of a paisley design, and a welcomingly plush cushion, while its still-lissome mechanisms produced a silent rocking. A sewing basket sat just to its left, which she regarded approvingly.

Moments later, the china clinked deliciously as Greta handed her the tea. "Be careful not to burn yourself," she said, then disappeared toward the back of the shoe, in search of clean gauze and tinctured antiseptics. And perhaps a moment of peace.

Lilith blew little puffs into the cup, savoring the heady aroma. Against the west wall stood a grandfather clock, its hickory surface striated with the worn, tiny paths of a sharp-nailed rodent. Below, in no particular order about the floor, sat a dozen mousetraps baited with morsels of cheddar. None of them was sprung.

She glanced expectantly at the clock's face, painted with a rather unsettling depiction of a cow in some kind of lunar orbit. The hands were about to strike the hour.

It was nearly time.

Suddenly reminded of something, Lilith straightened out her better leg and pushed herself up and out of the chair, then quickly hobbled to the oak hutch ensconcing her cherished porcelain egg collection. She opened the cabinet and quickly gathered up her treasures into a receiving pouch she'd made from a slip of her robe, then shuffled over to a distant cedar trunk, which she opened and therein delicately deposited the items, one at a time, upon a quilt sewn by a relative long dead, and whose name she could no longer remember.

Winded somewhat, she limped back to her chair. There, she took a moment to remind herself that with age comes wisdom, and it was an utter fool who did not see the landscape changing. The once heavy and enduring vintage atmosphere of a quaint existence had been sucked out, now replaced by a lighter, crisper, cleaner air, free of those particulates that amounted to so much ...disingenuousness.

Then she disappeared into a dark, recent memory...

* * *

Pinned to the ground, a black dagger securing each splayed arm, Lilith stared defiantly into those eight eyes. "Just make it quick, you filthy bugger!"

A guffaw. "You look like something that crawled away from some distant and unforgiving autumn," the Spider observed. "Something parched and in search of chlorophyll." He tilted in, as if attempting to gain a better focus. "Why I even bother-"

"Then why do you?" she spat.

The Spider seemed to suckle upon this bit of insolence. Then he said, "Tell me, do you keep that vinegar in a flask and close to your breast?" He thought another moment. "Yes," he decided as he inched even closer, "perhaps such guile might work to my advantage. And well to your salvation."

Lilith stared uncertainly, hopefully then, into those black marbles. "A favor, I'm guessing?"

* * *

Greta returned from the shadowy recesses of the shoe, her stride somewhat stilted, hesitant; her arms limp at her sides, her possession free of any medicinal supplies. She was staring out from behind a puzzled expression.

Lilith looked up from her reverie. "Why, dear, you look as if you've just discovered something most perplexing."

"I...the back door has been secured from the inside. Fortified with...spun silk... The staircase, too, prohibiting access to...to the upper chambers."

Lilith nodded that she understood, then retrieved her cup and saucer from the tray table alongside. She sipped quietly, reservedly, as if having returned to some kind of relevant contemplation.

Now Greta was gaping at the oak hutch; at all of the empty little pedestals within. "What ...what has happened to your beautiful eggs? They were there just moments ago-"

"I had to move them, dear. There's sure to be quite the commotion, and I didn't feel it prudent to leave them in its potential path."

Greta was now wringing her hands; her eyes displaying an alarming wideness. "A commotion? Of what sort?"

Lilith didn't answer, just kept sipping.

Something large just then went skittering by the kitchen window; a sickeningly lurid frolic of branching appendages.

Then, at the front door, an urgent tapping.

Lilith raised her eyes to the sound. "Just one moment, please," she requested of the caller.

Fixed in place, Greta was nonetheless searching anxiously for a way out: a window, another door-

"The bite was really just a teeny nip," Lilith confessed, "a warning of what was to come if I didn't hold up my end of the deal." She shrugged. "And to facilitate some subterfuge, to be sure."

Greta's knees and shoulders were now experiencing an affliction of tremors. "You sold me out to the Spider?"

"Oh, let's call it what it is, dear: a sacrifice. Just as were those naughty little kittens."

"I don't...understand. I've long been your friend. I take care of you, bathe you-"

"I'm sorry, dear. I really am. But we've been withering on the vine, all of us here. Nobody reads us anymore, and those that do don't take us seriously. So it's time to stop the pretenses." She sighed. "I've often wondered if perhaps that was the reason for the brevity of our individual stories. Yours, for instance, is but one stanza. I used to think that your tale was to simply illustrate the universal fear of arachnids, and mine the consequences children must face when guilty of bad behavior. But, perhaps the shortness of our stories is evidence only of their lacking, of their incompleteness."

"Incompleteness?"

"Why, yes, dear. They were left unfinished so that history might eventually shore them up; that their vagueness might finally surrender to those starker inevitabilities that we have for so long only insinuated." She returned her tea cup and saucer to the portable stand. "Yes, I'm afraid change is in the air." She cackled some more. "That is, for everyone except the Spider." She shook a crooked finger. "He will always have but one role; his lines forever memorized."

As a path of wetness blossomed downward upon Greta's pant leg, Lilith reached into the nearby sewing bag and pulled out a pair of darning needles, then a bolt of sienna colored wool. She began to maneuver her sentences as deftly as she crocheted the yarn. "Our dawns were but quaint utterances; but what shimmer upon our sunsets are harsher ramblings. Diatribes, I should think, against the insincerities."

Amid her own quaking terror, Greta noticed something perhaps even more terrifying than what awaited her on the other side of the door. "Your occasional rhyme...it's-"

"Gone, gone, gone!" Lilith shook her head. "Haven't you been listening? From now onward there will be no more rhyming, no more paying allegiance. Our country's dead, so should be its anthem."

Greta could only stare. Then, pitifully remembering her earlier promise, she entreated, "But ...Wee Willie Winkie's place." Her breaths had grown quicker, sharper; her voice now a crackling cellophane version of its former self. "How...how will you make the meeting?"

Lilith clucked disapprovingly. "My poor, poor dear. Not only are you a self-loathing bitch, but you're also not a very bright one," she said, punctuating the remark with an exaggerated crocheted loop.

Now the hitches; the threatening sob. "He'll do you like he did me,"

Greta warned, pointing at the door. "He's a liar, and not to be trusted. I am your proof – this act about to be committed against me - that he will renege on his promise."

"I know, dear. I know very well. But I'll advance a proposition of my own: I shall offer him the whereabouts of my children." Her lips formed a vile, crooked grin. "But just one at a time. By portioning them out, I'll be assured a very long reprieve. For, as you know, I have so many, many children."

Then Lilith raised her voice to the door, and said, finally, "Come in."

*("Wednesday's Child" was previously published in "Father Grim's Storybook"
(Wicked East Press; May 2012) under the pseudonym Jon-Michael Emory)*

The Job That Needed Doing

By Jack Granath

He didn't speak his first word until the afternoon of his third birthday, when he groaned a disappointed syllable at the grandmother bearing gifts and was punished. At least, that's the story attached to him and told at each subsequent birthday. He didn't really believe it. He didn't believe it because he didn't believe in what he didn't remember, and, with dire consequences for his personality, he didn't remember much of anything. Memories bounced off him like rain from a plastic tarp. Though he wasn't stupid, he retained almost none of what he learned. The continual ebb and flow of knowledge didn't bother him in the least, either. He moved through a mystifying world, checking things twice, doubting every encounter. He was not, in fact—despite the plain proof of various certificates—entirely sure of his own name, John Wayne Jr., because everybody called him Baby. His father was not named John Wayne. That's a different story.

He was now thirty-eight years old and worked in an office. He could not have told you what he did, exactly. The firm traded in financial advice, and he explained the company's policies, already adequately explained in a small brochure, to the clients. If these clients had actual questions—something to do, say, with money or math—he referred them to those who knew. Math was not his bag, though he had been asked not to say so to the clients. He had also been asked not to call himself Baby, but sometimes he broke that rule.

Ignorance of his own job description did not prevent him from applying for a promotion and a raise. He received neither, and a few days later his boss, a woman several years younger than he and much more attractive, asked him to wear the pig suit. He accepted her strategic explanation, that he was the only one big enough, despite obvious and pervasive evidence to the contrary.

The event was a fundraiser. What kind (kids with cancer or vicious old bigots in a lodge) he never learned, but he knew the company did this sort of thing. He guessed that when they didn't want to give money, they farmed out the pig, but he couldn't be sure. Maybe they sent in the pig when they *did* give money, as a kind of advertisement, a way of ensuring that their generous presence was known.

The suit itself was made of plush or, what's more likely, a plushy polyester fiber. Temperatures inside could reach one hundred and twenty-five degrees. Performers wore a special vest with pockets for ice packs in order to survive. No one knew what the head was made of. It was an enormous thing, maybe six or seven times larger than a properly proportioned pig's head. The material looked like papier-mâché but had stood up in several heavy rains. The general consensus tended toward plastic, but judging by the weight of the thing, Baby settled on wood and clay.

One of the unwritten rules governing the pig suit was that, if you wore it once, you would be asked to wear it again. Baby's friend Ted compared it to having sex in prison. (Ted let Baby call him "my friend Ted" in return for a considerable amount of menial office labor.) At any rate, wearing the suit became a regular part of Baby's routine.

Ted was not the only one to make mean-spirited comparisons. Most in the department teased Baby about it, and all of them whispered behind his back. The friendly ones told him he was doing a good job "under the circumstances" or "all things considered" and, torturing their own semi-professional work ethic, commended him for doing a job that needed doing.

But Baby didn't see it as a job that needed doing. He saw it as an adventure in self-reflection. Fitting the giant head over his real head was like snapping on the bubble of a space suit. Sensory experience changed at that moment, all sounds being muted except his breathing, which seemed exaggerated and echoing. He liked to feel the ice packs cooling him while sweat dripped down his nose. He liked the smell of the unidentifiable materials. If he could have reached the inner wall of the great head with his tongue, he would have, but he had tried and failed. He even liked the fact that, once he put on the head, he was basically blind. The only openings were the nostrils at the end of the snout. Looking out at the world through these nostrils was like playing a game with wrapping-paper tubes. He had to be led around by the hand.

Blindness made him so alive to what remained of his senses, though, that he wondered if it was really necessary. There lay the hidden reward, this intimation of extra-human abilities. After spending some time in the suit, the boundary between his own identity and the pig's grew blurry. He felt like a lumbering creature with a towering balloon head, and it was a nice change.

Ted had to craft his jokes without reference to any of these invisible currents. He saw a much simpler dynamic behind Baby's complaisance — the psychology of pride. The pig suit was a uniform, and men like to wear uniforms. Navy SEALs like them, crossing guards like them, and guys in pig suits like them too. To complicate things, Baby fell in love. Lacking imagination and common sense, he aimed his affections at an office mate named Gloria Brookbottom, who wore stiletto heels and preferred firemen. He had convinced himself, from what he interpreted as a longing look on her part, that she found his "special assignments" impressive.

The company was constantly hiring and firing people. Baby couldn't understand why. One day his pretty boss mentioned that a recent hire had some experience in acting or puppetry or something and might relieve Baby of the task. She kidded him with the ironic supposition that he wouldn't give it up without a fight. Baby didn't get the joke and silently agreed with her.

The new guy's name was Joe. He chaffed Baby in words borrowed from their boss and got control of the suit by the end of the week. Baby dug his heels in, and the tug of war began.

Somehow, Joe was able to wear the pig suit without suffering the pig-suit stigma. He was a decent guy and everyone liked him. His experience in acting (or puppetry) marked him as a pleasant eccentric and made pig-suit duty okay. In fact, his co-workers actively sought his approval, hoping that a bit of intimacy with a bohemian like that (but a normal bohemian, a nice drinking-buddy bohemian) would argue against the obvious meaninglessness of their lives. Also, word leaked back to the office that he did one hell of a job in that suit. He didn't just throw it on and shuffle back and forth. He gestured and posed and preened. Sometimes he danced.

Baby saw to it that he got his fair share of time in the suit, but the contest was weighing on him. He began to have strange dreams in which he was a giant pig. Actually, "pig" is the wrong word. He was what he was when he wore the suit, only it wasn't a suit, it was him. On the other hand, sometimes it wasn't him. Sometimes he was only a witness to the activities of this pig-suit creature. In one dream, for instance, he watched the giant polyester pig stand in front of a urinal, relieve himself loudly, and groan. In another, he, as the suit incarnate, sat on a bench and smoked cigarettes with a Salvation Army Santa Claus. They told racist jokes and laughed.

He knew he needed a vacation, but taking one at this point would be too dangerous. Joe's reputation was growing. Even Gloria Brookbottom made time for Joe, and this bothered Baby more than anything else. They competed for her attention in the same way they did for the suit, and Baby knew he was losing both battles. One night he dreamed that he, the pig, received a magnificently sensuous scalp massage from a giant, lime-green lizard. The hugeness of his head multiplied the ecstasy. It felt like miles of intensely tactile pleasure balanced perfectly on the fulcrum of his brain. Without guilt, he reached around to grope her fuzzy flanks. Then, by way of a contorted dream anatomy, he was running his hooves along her plush back and shoulders. When he woke up, he knew that it was Gloria. Sitting at his desk the next day, he thought of her and realized he was crying.

Later, he wore the pig suit for a group of children. As usual, he had no inkling of the event's basic purpose. The location was a grade-school gymnasium with very low basketball hoops. He knocked his huge head against one of them early on, but things went better after that. The rumor that Joe could strut and dance in the suit, whereas Baby could barely walk, was slander. Long ago Baby had introduced a couple of dance steps (though careful, shuffling ones) into his routine. That night he let it all hang out. He was doing it for Gloria, though she was not, of course, there. The boundary between his Baby self and his pig self had never felt so evanescent. He grew absurdly confident, tried impossible things, and accomplished them. Toward the end of the evening, with the ice packs largely melted and his head buzzing from exhaustion, he attempted the Sailor's Hornpipe and kicked some kid in the throat.

He didn't wear the suit so much after that. He slinked around the office, sheepish and defeated, conscious, above all, that he had disappointed Gloria. His friend Ted was merciless in his mockery, which made of the slightly embarrassing story something like an eternal flame. People he barely knew ribbed him in the elevator weeks after the event. Meanwhile, Joe ascended the throne. He developed a following of cheering children. He posed with the governor. He was praised in a memo.

A rumor went around that Joe and Gloria had gone on a date. Another one went that Joe had come up with a way of picking a simple tune on the banjo while dressed in the pig suit, a feat that Baby knew to be impossible. He welcomed the plain lie because it helped him dismiss the first story, which he found tragically plausible, along with it.

Occasionally, of course, emergencies arose, and Baby had to wear the suit. All of the pleasure had gone out of it, though. He felt like an invader, a cat burglar, a parasite. He felt like what he was, a man dressed in another man's pig suit. None of this kept him from dreaming of a comeback. He saw himself moving a crowd of children more deeply than any banjo-playing son of a bitch ever could. The superior virtue of his understated style would be acknowledged. The governor would need his services desperately, at the last minute, and Baby would be there.

Baby sensed that Joe didn't like him wearing the suit. It was Ted who planted the poisonous idea in his brain. He suggested that audiences might mistake Baby's child-abusing performances for Joe's off days. Soon after, Baby noticed that the key to the closet where they kept the suit was missing. Joe had taken it home "by mistake." Later, Baby had to perform in tennis shoes, because the detachable foot covers ("hoofsies," he thought of them) were, at Joe's bidding, being cleaned. It was clearly a case of sabotage.

Apart from glaring at Joe every chance he got, Baby kept this knowledge to himself. He concentrated on other things, locating the main obstacle to his comeback in the compromised nature of the boards he was permitted to strut upon. Whenever a major event was scheduled, Joe materialized at their boss's elbow, ready to suit up. When Baby had a chance at all, it was sure to involve something like a retirement home or a ladies luncheon. He was the second stringer on the football team—with this difference, though: the "season" had no end. Given enough "big games," he knew, he would eventually be called upon to play.

The call came late on a Friday afternoon. The pig was to make an appearance at the symphony's summer fundraiser. Dates were switched, communications botched, and Joe out of town. Their boss ran around frantic and actually shouting, until Baby soothed her by volunteering. He spoke to her with absurd confidence, in a deep voice. Whether she fell under his spell or gave it up as the best she could do, she calmed down, gave him his instructions, and left for the day. It was then that he discovered the ice packs were missing.

He pulled everything from the freezer in the break room, unearthing a Cool Whip container marked "1996," but no ice packs. Joe had stung him again. The ice packs weren't ordinary ones, either. They were made to fit the vest. Running out and buying some was not an option. He considered using the frozen peas he found behind the Cool Whip, but one of his co-workers eyed him telepathically, and he put them back.

It was a hot night. His coup would be that much more heroic. He arrived at the music hall to learn that he would be stationed at the top of a huge and famous flight of stairs. They were trying to get the air-conditioners working.

He changed into the pig suit in a small room off the top landing. As soon as he snapped his head into place, he felt the temperature start to climb. A small girl in a white dress, one of those who sold bonbons at intermission, was to be his guide. In her free hand she clutched a miniature violin.

Baby stood on that landing and waved for forty-five minutes. Everyone was coming up the clearly marked entrance-side of the staircase, because people at symphonies are well behaved. Baby stood at the top of the exit-side. Under the cheerful head, his mouth was hanging open, his face red as a rubber ball. Sweat was pouring out of him as if he had hot rocks in there. At some point, he could no longer tell if he was still holding the hand of the little girl. Then he wondered if he was still waving. He felt that he was floating, not up exactly, but up and a little over. It would have been a pleasant sensation except for the horrible effects of heat exhaustion. He tried to shake it off and get his bearings, but instead he fainted.

That famous flight of stairs: ninety marble steps in sets of thirty, separated by two broad landings. He almost came to rest at the far edge of the first but, after teetering a moment at the brink, spilled over and down to the next one, where he went the distance again. Needless to say, the steady stream of those coming up on the entrance-side stopped to watch the lone, porcine figure descending toward the exit. A few of the ladies synchronized a sharp sucking sound, but apart from that there was silence—the kind of silence that only symphony-goers can create—except for the clattering and the crashing of the pig.

He was not badly hurt. He probably would have survived Niagara Falls in that suit. A panicky usher dragged him by his diminutive tail into the coat room. There a managerial sort, clearly concerned about insurance, revived him. He was thrilled to find that Baby could walk and helped him out to the car.

That was the end of Baby's days in the pig suit. No one said so, and no one had to. His boss would sometimes ask, vaguely, who was going to wear the suit to this or that function, as if she were too busy to decide. Ted kept at his jokes, knowing instinctively, however, not to touch the subject of the great fall. Even Joe suggested, once or twice, that Baby get back in the game. But he did not. The fall had changed him. He stalked around the office glaring at people. On one occasion he told Gloria Brookbottom to "stuff it." And he was weirdly terrified of the pig suit itself, viewing it as an instrument of torture he had been tested with and survived.

The fact is that Baby was not unconscious during the fall. True, he fainted at the top of the steps, but only to come to, in an almost metaphysically disoriented way, a few bounces later. He passed out again at the bottom of the steps, believing that the cessation of his whirling journey meant death. He succumbed to it. He faced death and agreed. The experience changed his understanding of the present moment, which he now saw as something radically less stable than he formerly thought. He had always been a confused and suspicious man except, briefly, in the isolation tank of that pig suit, which had a healing effect on his spirit. But he was poisoned with his own medicine now and fled it like one enlightened to the horrors of an accepted but primitive practice.

A couple of months later, Baby got fired. He had continued to dispatch his vague duties adequately, but the firm merged with another one, and his new bosses, after taking stock of their personnel resources, were puzzled by his existence. They made rows and columns and scratched their heads and let him go. Soon thereafter, Baby got religion in a serious and self-destructive way and found a job, on the business end of things, in a church. He married a large, young woman of great childbearing potential and turned out a kid a year for the next six. The non-appearance of numbers seven and younger was not for lack of trying, either. His long-suffering wife simply learned a bit of subterfuge.

What exactly went through his head, between the great fall and the great sowing, will never be known, but as his pastor once put it, "It went through funny." Time had something to do with the transformation, that much is clear. Viewing the present moment as a sort of hideout—a natural strategy since earliest childhood—no longer seemed like an effective defense against the demands and confusions of life. He was shoring up his experience with things that would come after it, even if he was incapable of concentrating on them for more than a few minutes at a time — even if, as in the case of God, "concentration" meant picturing something from a Saturday-morning cartoon. He liked to watch cartoons, though some of them made him nervous. Sometimes, watching them, he'd whimper, and his children would have to comfort him. Sometimes, he'd just get up and leave.

Removal

By Elizabeth Dadabo

Your skeleton is bursting out of you at the seams, throbbing insistently, stabbing you from the inside. You are trying to fall sleep. You want to pull every bone out of your body and lay all 208 of them in neat order, bolt them together at the joints, and display them on your wall for guests to marvel at, with a mixture of fascination and disinterest. You wistfully imagine your newfound popularity, and probably fame, once you've achieved this impossible, awful task.

Your slumbering boyfriend won't be awakened. He passed out more than two hours ago, his back turned to you. His breathing is labored yet steady, the sound of deep slumber. You stare off into the darkness of your closet for a moment, a finite space in daylight hours, yet limitless, liminal in the dark – and in that space you devise your plan of action. Finally, you get up and head silently through the bedroom door, and into the kitchen.

You pour a glass of cold, filtered water from the pitcher in the refrigerator, drink it down, and follow that by eating two small pieces of crunchy chocolate. You consider a drag off the bottle of whiskey on the counter to numb the pain, then decide against it. You want to feel everything. A slight moan emanates from the bedroom as you open the kitchen drawer to retrieve the steak knives. After laying a set of thick, fluffy white towels on the glass coffee table, you prepare your toolset to begin work. The most logical beginning point is the ribs. Cutting with the longest of the knives, you insert the blade just above your belly, to remove your bottom right rib.

The knife goes in much easier than you thought, and there's so little blood, which is equally surprising. Dabbing at the entry point with gauze, you don't have to apply serious pressure, or cauterize the wound. You take a pair of forceps - tweezers, really - and force them inside the slit you made with your knife, grab hold of your rib at the base, wiggle, wiggle, and pull. The bone cracks away from your spine, hanging in stasis above your liver. You must now grab its tip, through the same cut, and pull it out. You have to be extremely careful not to damage your internal organs. You need those.

The rib comes out at last, popping through fat and skin with a satisfying squish, and the rest is a slow, careful guiding outward, pressing on your belly at just the right moments, pushing the formerly encapsulated bone into the open air. You place the prize on one of the towels on your glass table, in the spot you've laid out for it. Then, for the most part, it's extremities inward. Of course, you leave your spine and arms for last. The most difficult part is removing your own skull while keeping your face and brain intact. The process is a literally impossible one, yet somehow, you manage it. And you never even went to medical school.

Your emptying skin goes through the motions of pulling each bone out, one by one, going more and more limp, muscle and blood and vessels still intact. Your vascular system is pumping acutely, each press of your heartbeat carrying with it a novel, exquisite agony. Your organs are functioning as before, your brain is thinking, although with no skull to knock around inside.

Once you've shed you skeleton, placed the bones in order, cleaned them, tagged them, labeled them, and ordered them, you are ready to assemble the masterpiece. Your hands, now loose flesh, are almost useless in the process, and your entire body is shaking uncontrollably. You're not sure how you make it through, hinging your skeleton, glueing, testing for flexibility, tautness. You want to give up at almost every point; your brain, still sending signals to your muscle tissue, jolts your senses into rebellion at least once each minute. Determination overtakes the urge to reduce pain, however, and you remain steadfast. When you are done, you gaze at your handiwork with a mixture of satisfaction, grief and horror. Your skeleton is perfectly arranged.

It is so much more difficult to move without bones. Yet once you begin, momentum carries you. And it hurts. More than you thought it ever could, or would. It's as though the pain of the entire world is shooting through every surface, every cell, in your body. Logic told you that you would die without bones. But you're not dead, just in agony. Dutifully, you bear down through the terror of this pain as if there were never another option. And perhaps there wasn't.

You begin to walk, your feet wobbling, legs deeply unsteady, top heavy without your femurs to load your bottom half. You feel empty, oozing, wiggly. Steadying yourself after every step, your torso flails forward and back, your head leading in unpredictable directions. You swoon with the pressure drop of each chaotic sway. Your brain rests indelicately on top of your soft palate, where your jaw once was. The weight tests the loading capacity of the flexible tissue, which you never thought had any imaginative generativity of its own, but a new burden creates an animal form of consciousness, the ache of frustration, loss.

Your organs: liver, gall bladder, stomach, intestines, kidneys, rest at the base of your belly. There is more sinew, tissue, viscera, to hold them in place than in your head. You can still think, shockingly clearly, with pain underwriting every instant, stretching even the most imperceptible fractions of time into parsed eternities. Where is it you're going again? Just walking. Take your bones out, go walking, come back home, fall asleep. That will help with this insomnia.

Shuffling out the front door, you exit the back gate hesitantly, shutting it as carefully, as you can, but you lose your grip, and it shuts with a crash, wrought iron door against metal frame. The alley is pitch black, save for a single garage light twenty yards ahead. As you advance, you hear a noise behind you. A scritching. It must be a rat, come out of concrete and mud to eat your unstable carcass, to make off with a toe or a chunk of shin and scuttle back to its hidey-hole. You turn, slowly, to see what it is behind you, dreading the maw of a hostile animal, its incisors and hunger, but your pursuer makes a deft move to the right and ducks out of view before you can determine its size or shape.

As you turn back to your left, you see something running across the alley, towards the park near your apartment – it's your skeleton, running at a full clip, arms pumping, on the balls of its feet – footfalls silent, perfect, Olympian... Shock gives way to a desperate, desolate sadness. Were you holding it back? Were you literally dead weight?

Momentarily, you forget your excruciating pain and make your way towards the park, to pause and watch it for a while. It seems to want to stick to the field, not venture out into the neighborhood or towards the lagoon – the floodlights surrounding the baseball diamond make it shine luminously white. Observing greedily, you feel the longing and vague resentment with which one views a photograph of a movie star, an old lover, or someone else's puppy dog.

It stands momentarily, collecting itself, outstretches its right arm, and follows with a spin in the gravel. It begins to dance, pirouetting from first to third base, and adds several jetés to reach home base, where it stands, preening itself by brushing dust away, checking its ankles for gravel. These are the things you could never do while your skeleton was in your skin, and certainly won't be able to do now. How you tried; to make your body into a graceful apparatus, pointed toes and muscular legs and all, futile dance classes with hands over feet, tailbone tucked and toes turned out in fifth position, and now your skeleton can do it all effortlessly, with perfect technique, as if it's mocking you. But it doesn't have feelings, or sensation – or so you thought. Your skeleton seems to be telling you that you grotesquely misjudged it.

It disappears from view, after taking a light-footed, two-legged leap. You watch for it, waiting for it to emerge behind your back. Pain emerges again after the wave of betrayal-induced adrenaline spikes and recedes. You forgot that your organs are floating around in an ether of tissue and goo, and now your toes are shriveling up like dirty raisins, curl under and press into the balls of your feet, your eyes are popping out of your head. Where your skeleton is graceful, articulate, firm, you are inchoate, a cluster of undifferentiated masses, raw nerves and chemical signals - clumsy, and frail.

You walk towards the baseball diamond, your tongue lolling, your heart sinking between your lungs and toward your liver. You want to rest, to collapse in a heap like goose-bumped chicken skin, to leave your carcass for pickpockets and mushrooms. You imagine being covered over with maggots and fungus, you wonder what it would be like to breathe your last, or just to sleep. How your lungs would expand and contract with no ribcage. How your dreams would be filled with apocalyptic scenes, non sequitur childhood memories.

You sit down on a park bench. It is not so simple as those seven words. Sitting is more like slithering, you are becoming more and more a human slug, inching your way across the piece of public furniture, leaving a trail of slime, feeling pieces of old gum dent your tender skin – sharp-faced pink stones scraping at your insides. You clamber, feeling persecuted by gravity and time. You know, though, that you are to blame. You sit, finally, and await the return of your beloved. You never realized how much you loved your skeleton. You weep, tears oozing out of your porous and dusty ducts, pushing your eyes perilously closer to popping all of the way out of your head.

It doesn't return. It's headed off to a tavern, downing pints of beers it could never drink while your brain was making the decisions, and turning its eyeless sockets, *your* eyeless sockets, towards some of the pub's denizens, drunken urchins in need of companionship or public solitude. It's locked in an embrace with some pathetic bastard who is emptying the contents their soul and their stomach in alternate volleys, verifying lusts, love, hatreds and allegiances between rounds of darts and bouts of tears. Your sympathetic skeleton can't get drunk.

Vanity is the quality your skeleton most freely embodies. It will be forever thin and young. You are a miasma of regret, contaminating public spaces. You wonder how it is holding itself together, though. Those complex, balletic movements weren't the stuff of a detached set of bones. Its performance replays in your head, like a mimeograph spitting out endless copies. It was so beautiful, so infuriating. *Why* wouldn't your skeleton ever behave that way when you enervated it? If you had only known you might not have gone this far. Frankenstein's Monster was less stubborn. You feel cheated out of the beauty that your skeleton possessed, duped by its pretended lethargy, shamed by your lack of understanding of its true nature. You imagined that if you asked why it withheld these talents from you, it would cock its skull to the side, look at your empty skin with a half-pitying, half-condescending look, its jaw clattering wordlessly, its hands gesticulating silently, playfully. It would mock you, again, with perfectly articulated movements.

This walk has felt long, though it has been short. The longer you ooze, the more the base of your leg expands each time it hits the pavement. This sensation is discomfiting, painful at first – then you realize that it offers a measure of stability. It expands, bears the load that your femur once did. And you come to a realization – just as your skeleton adapted quickly to its open air digs, so your muscles and skin begin to imagine a way out of their predicament. And you can never return home again.

Your movements are lurching, halting at first, but after a few blocks, take on a smoothness and certainty of their own. Your boneless skin does a monstrous tango across the backlit pavement. Head hanging backwards, over your shoulders, your arms and torso pitch forward, making their way towards the ground. It will be easier, now, to walk on all fours. Just as your toeless feet expand and contract with each step, so now your boneless fingers discover new versatility. Spreading like the feet of a tree frog, they absorb the weight of your body into your fingertips, broadening them and providing a platform to launch yourself forward.

You are becoming your truest self. Your skeleton has realized that it's better off without you, and you are a four-limbed cephalopod. You lurch your way through the park. A group of teenagers smoking weed doesn't see you in the midst of their intoxication and laughter, but one, a short kid wearing thick black-framed glasses and a Bulls jersey, gawks, and yells, "Hey man, what the fuck is THAT?" Another chimes in, "Shit, it's just a loose dog, leave it the fuck alone." But biggest fan isn't having any of that, "No man, that ain't no dog. It looks like a fucking alien or something. " He's walking towards your scuttling form, and you try to lurch faster, but he's gaining on you, and he kicks you with a swift movement that sends you reeling. "What the fuck *is* this thing, man?"

You try to speak, to say, "I'm a human", but it comes out "Garf flaf verlufen." You're not even sure that's equivalent in jaw-less humanoid cephalopod. "Shit, it *talks!*" The kid says. You can tell he feels a bad for kicking you, but also a scared, and contemptuous. He reaches for something, and at first you're thinking it's gun, or a knife, but it's a lighter. He takes another puff off of a green glass bowl, and kicks you again, this time, more lightly, almost as if to test your reaction. You say, "Please don't!" But it comes out "Reeelph nobe!" And you squirt a black cloud of ink from between your thighs. "Aagh!" The kid yells. He pulls back to hit you with the stick, once again, but you've summoned some strength from some deep well within, and slunk off down a hill, and after tripping yourself up a bit on some underbrush, you are upon a lagoon.

You slip in, former fingers first, barely making a ripple, and the water is freezing. Your clothes are sticking to your expanding and contracting limbs, and you can hear the footfalls of the kid, looking for revenge. "It fucking covered me in this shit, man!" "Are you sure you didn't just shit yourself, Liam?" "Do I fucking look like I shit myself? The fucker squirted me with black ink!" You can't help but let out a yawp, of fright, of satisfaction. At least you're not dead, you're not the one humiliated. But you are, increasingly, no longer human. Your eyes peer out from the top of the water, your legs expand and contract just below the surface. You breath through your nose, your mouth is beginning to seal itself, toothless and useless, you make your way towards the center of the lagoon, where they won't be able to see you, or so you hope. "Where the fuck did it go?" Liam intones, plaintively and angrily. "It was just a fucking dog, man. " Another, taller, fatter, says. "You're *such* a fucking LIAR dude!" A third claps Liam on the back, contemptuously.

For a second, you feel sorry for Liam, I mean, you know what it's like, to be called a liar just for seeing something no one else can see. But, fuck him, he was trying to hurt you. The group of boys runs around the lagoon, searching for the fucked-up dog that squirted Liam with smelly black shit, a mixture of blood and bile. They want to harm you. For being fucked up. For being unable to speak. For being something between animal, human and alien. And you want to die, too, but not at their hands. Not their way. A streetlamp is illuminating you, now. Or the moon. It's directly on top of your head, making you a beacon. You leave the center of the lagoon, and hide among a cluster of rocks. The boys have split up now, they are seeking you out, probably to kill you for sport. You try to make yourself invisible, silent, wrapping your limbs around the base of a rock, when you feel something grab you.

"I got it!" One of them chimes. It's not Liam. His teeth and eyes are gleaming in the moonlight, and he's grabbing you by the paw/arm/

tentacle. You try and wriggle away, you try and squirt ink, but all you can do is pull, and without your bones, your afraid he'll pull your hand off, and you'll bleed out. You allow him to pull you out of the water, and he throws you on the embankment, looking you over. "Shit, man, little dude was right, this *ain't* no dog." He looks disgusted. You are wet, slimy, hairy, limp. "Fuck this thing. Take it out of its misery." A tall, skinny kid in a black coat says, grabbing a stick. All your sealed-shut mouth can muster is "EEEEEEEEGH."

Something knocks the stick out of his hand. With a swift kick, your skeleton has emerged to protect you from these park vigilantes. The kid brandishes a pocketknife, swinging it at your skeleton, who recoils from it, pulling its chest in and jumping backwards like an expert fencer. It does a cartwheel and grabs your assailant by the wrist, flipping him over his head. Your skeleton doesn't want anyone to get hurt. But they will. Seeing they're fighting a skeleton, the kids scatter, muttering about some sort of curse. Liam tries to bash its skull with a rock, but misses and falls flat on his face. Your skeleton backhands one of them, knocks another to the ground with a kick to the chest, and picks your skin up and starts running.

It's so fast. You're draped over its shoulders, and the joy you feel is overwhelming. You're reunited, and your skeleton is running just as before the park, just as graceful, as silent, and perfect. It feels, for an instant, like you are your old self again, only better, faster, more – then you feel the drab dripping of your tentacles against the bones, the drag of your raisin-y toes against the pavement and grass, and you know that it is not so. Overwhelming sadness overtakes you, bulging eyeballs resting in the crook of your skeleton's neck, in a turgid embrace, you begin to sob, disgusting, phlegmy snot pouring from what used to be your nose.

Your skeleton grabs your feet and wraps them around its ribcage, and you are secure, still soaked, but able to join it in flight. It pirouettes and jetés, cartwheels and flips, it triple sow-kows and spins once, twice, three times in the air, and sticks every landing. Your pleasure is both vicarious and personal. You aren't reproaching your skeleton for running off on you any more. All you've every really wanted is total freedom, total joy. And for this moment, it is yours.

Your skeleton has stopped its acrobatics. Suddenly, you realize that it is running for the lake. You know it means to leave you there, to let you drift out as far as you might go. This is your fate, eternal separation. You chose. What other outcome could there have been? What other possible future? What alternate past? Desperately, you hang on to your ribcage, and this time it is your skeleton who has to extract you. Being a slippery eel, though, you have knotted and tied yourself around each rib in an indecipherable pattern. Jumping into the water, your skeleton dives ten feet below its surface, swimming farther and farther from the embankment. You hang on, fiercely, squeezing every muscle, until you are forced to choose hanging on or death. So you let go. Defiantly, you squirt your skeleton with a giant cloud of ink as you make your way to the surface, angry, deeply hurt.

About half a mile from shore, you come to the surface to breathe. The skyline of the city visible, but no longer illuminates the water's surface at this distance. You hear nothing but the sound of your own swimming. You've never felt so desperate, so alone. At least in the lagoon you could have had some sort of company, ducks and fish, kids and dogs. It would have been a better home, except for those goddamned kids. You never would have had to worry about food, maybe you could have even taken a walk around the park occasionally, when no one was looking. You come back to yourself, in the lake, and you come back to your skeleton, which you can make out, swimming back to shore, about 5 yards away. It waves goodbye to you. It's not mocking you. It's over. It continues its trek back to shore, in perfect breaststrokes, slowly, as you lurch your way north, up the shoreline, to who-knows-where.

Impala

By Timothy O'Leary

I was eleven years old when the man took us. It was my fault.

Mom made clear we were to be home no later than five, even making us repeat "five o'clock" as if time were a foreign language. But at five-thirty my little brother Dennis and I were in the arcade in the back of Sunset Bowling Alley, feet glued in place by Ms. Pac-Man's blue and yellow glow. Dennis whined every few minutes, anticipating Mom's fury, but there is no free will between little and big brothers. Finally, spurred by Ms. Pac-Man's gulping sound track and the violent applause of bowling balls cracking pins, I reached level twenty-eight, the highest score in the history of that particular game, nodded as I entered my signature—GOD—into the name space in the top slot, and called it quits.

As we were leaving, I noticed the man, standing at the counter and handing in his bowling shoes. First it was the long stringy hair and tattered army field jacket that grabbed my attention, the street uniform of the Vietnam vets that had been roaming around the last few years. When he turned, his face gaunt, eyes half-lidded, I envisioned Bruce Dern, the man who killed John Wayne in *The Cowboys*. I didn't notice him follow us out, so I didn't know it was him who grabbed us as we unlocked our Huffys from the light pole, his boney fingers digging into the napes of our necks and rushing us like cattle through a chute into that deep car trunk.

Dennis cried out, and the man slapped him hard on a fat moist cheek, stunning us into submission.

"Shut the fuck up or I'll cut your goddamn head off," he said in a low serious voice. I wrapped my arm around my brother's face, urging him to be quiet as the lid slammed us into darkness. As the car moved onto the street we bounced hard on spongy shocks, damp rusty grit covering my cheek, air thick with oil and some other rotting smell. Sometimes I heard a muffled hum from the radio, Credence Clearwater Revival, the man singing along out-of-tune to *Fortunate Son*.

After maybe twenty minutes we stopped, the brakes grating. I heard him get out of the car, a garage door rolling up, then rolling back down after we'd moved in. When the trunk opened bright light streamed in, the terror subsiding momentarily. It was a garage like any other, a place where normal men like our dad stowed their stuff: a lawn mower in the corner, rakes and tools hanging neatly on pegs, a boxy freezer humming against the wall. But Dennis flew into a panic, springing out as if he might take flight, a bird locked for days in a room suddenly freed. The man grabbed him, yelled, "Shut the fuck up, I warned you," and slammed him down outside of my sight line. I collapsed at the front of the car, covering my eyes when the man grabbed the short, square-headed shovel off the wall, swinging it as if he were about to bust-up stubborn dirt clods.

Impala. I concentrated on the chrome emblem on the car's grill, trying to block out the sheaving sound, metal into thick mud, and the more horrible silence when my brother stopped screaming. The man rushed to the front of the car and grabbed me by the hair, bloody shovel dangling in his left hand, and dragged me into the basement.

And that was the last time I was above ground for nine years.

Thirty-three hundred days. Eighty thousand hours. Five million minutes. I had plenty of time to do the math, to learn every inch of that twelve-by-twelve room. Fresh hospital-green paint and gray linoleum, a new porcelain sink and toilet in the corner. I knew I wasn't the first. I crawled on the floor like a slug, forensically analyzing every inch of the walls, spent hours splayed on my back under the bed pretending the crisscross of the box springs were clouds. I imagined our family in Pioneer Park, our parents laughing as Dennis and I struggled to get a kite airborne. And it was there I discovered the person imprisoned before me. He—was it a he?—I always assumed so, had notched two hundred and forty-one scratches, four vertical with the fifth a cross scratch, on the metal slats. Did he escape? I wondered. Or was his time up? I counted days in my head until I could no longer keep track, panicking when I thought I might be close to that number.

Sometimes the man brought me comic books, and I'd pretend they were letters from home; Archie and Jughead updating me on what was happening with the gang in Riverdale. After maybe a year he started rolling in a black and white television for an hour or two every few days, just never at a time when I could see news or anything about the outside world. Reception was almost non-existent, but I'd twist and turn the rabbit ears to watch snowy episodes of Gilligan's Island, wishing I was trapped on an island instead of here, swinging in a hammock and eating coconuts with the Skipper. Sometimes the man would even watch with me. He'd hear me giggle, and slip in quietly to stand in the corner, a strange smile on his face as if he were witnessing something magical. He might even have cookies or chocolates wrapped in a napkin, and he'd cautiously hand me one, gesturing toward his lips as if I didn't know how to eat, then grin happily when I chewed and smiled at the sweetness.

After a while I couldn't comprehend time, didn't know how old I was or how long I'd been locked away. At some point the man gave me an electric razor and told me to shave every other day, though he wouldn't allow a mirror. My hands traced my face, the strange new sensation of whiskers, chubby cheeks now slim, trying to comprehend what I might look like.

I'd speak just to hear the changes in my voice as it grew deeper and foreign. Eventually, I forgot my parents and friends, my thoughts confined to Dennis and the one who'd made the notches. Praying I'd misunderstood what had transpired in the garage, I'd talk to my brother for hours on the off-chance that he might be in the next room with his ear to the wall. With a lot of time to think, you think a lot about time, and I often considered the importance of minutes. If only I'd followed my mother's instructions and left a few minutes earlier, we wouldn't be here. If it had taken me a few minutes longer to beat Ms. Pac-Man, the man wouldn't have seen us. Sometimes I'd lie under the bed and carry-on long discussions with the one who came before me, the only one who could really understand it all.

One day there was an explosion upstairs, rattling the foundation of the house like a tank had brought down a wall, followed by angry shouting. My door burst apart at the frame, a helmeted man in black, with what looked like a cannon swinging from his arms, yelling at me to get on the ground. The room filled with other uniformed men brandishing huge weapons. I couldn't comprehend what was happening and thought they might be aliens. Like *War of the Worlds*, perhaps the earth had been overrun by creatures from another planet and the man and I were the last holdouts. Had he actually been trying to save me?

They whisked me from the basement into a sinister-looking van, and for the next twenty-four hours I rotated between hospitals and a police station. I soon understood the truth. I was now a twenty-year-old man that had spent almost half his life in a cellar imagining he was friends with Veronica and Richie Rich, and communing with dead people.

My mother was gone. Some suspected suicide, Mom so grief stricken that late one night six years earlier she drove head-on into a telephone pole. My father had remarried, filled his house with new children, and after my initial homecoming he didn't seem overly interested in seeing me, an unexpected, painful relic from a time he'd rather forget.

I was famous for a few weeks, even appeared on the cover of People Magazine, "The Boy in the Basement." But horrifying stories like mine have a short shelf life, and I was soon replaced in the public's imagination by a British movie star caught communing with a male prostitute, and a Nebraska woman that gave birth two dozen times.

Society loves blame, and officials that should have found me right after the abduction lost their jobs. Friends and classmates I barely remembered, now in college or living their lives, threw a party and paraded me around like a science exhibit.

Of course there was counseling and concern but I felt more like a specimen, doctors repeatedly urging me to confront the worst details. Those that made their livings documenting monstrous crimes hovered around with the promise of fame and money, neither of which I craved. I had no desire to be the star of a freak show. I understood that everyone assumed a boy held in solitary confinement for half his life had to be insane, and people feared me almost as much as they did the man. I'd been branded.

I suppose I could have gone back to school or learned some kind of trade, but mostly I just wanted to keep moving. For a while I tried to relate, to be human, but the world didn't seem any more real than those comic books, and I found myself drawn to ugly places that reminded me of the room. The counselors and psychologists expressed a grim understanding of my choices, my hollowness. I was defined by my diagnosis: post-traumatic stress and sociopathic tendencies brought on by years of captivity. And I suppose that at some point even a compassionate society has to enforce its own rules and laws.

In Solvang, California I was arrested for assault and armed robbery. My victim only spent one night in the hospital, but it cost me a year in prison. Next they sent me to a halfway house and a job I refused to work, the hairnet and paper hat the last straw. I left for Texas, where they were less forgiving after I shoved a beer bottle into a man's ear, landing me in an even smaller room for three years. Colorado, four years for drugs and a stolen Glock. In Idaho I made a decent living robbing truck stops and convenience stores, racking up another half decade in an institution surrounded by fir trees. After that I worked my way back home to Montana, even though there was nobody there I wanted to see. That's where I went big time, seventy-five to life for killing a bartender in Great Falls. Did I feel remorse for the man I murdered, the people I hurt? They were no more real to me than those blue and yellow circles I used to gobble-up with Ms. Pac Man. I wasn't even sure I existed.

Montana has only one prison, Deer Lodge, a red-stoned fortress straight out of a medieval nightmare, built in 1871 as the territorial lock-up. You might've thought someone would do a little research, realize who I was, and decide it might not be a great idea to incarcerate me in the same joint as the man who kept me captive for all those years. Maybe they'd forgotten us. It had been over twenty years, and he was growing old serving three consecutive life sentences, locked-up in solitary when I arrived, so perhaps they thought it wouldn't be an issue. Might have even seen me as a solution, an easy way to trim the herd, assuming I would certainly kill him and save the taxpayers some money.

In my fifth year at Deer Lodge they released him back into general population. I spotted him across the yard, head down, smoking cigarettes and shuffling back and forth on a six foot stretch near the wall. He seemed smaller than I remembered. He had to be pushing sixty, skinny and frail, thin-stretched skin the color of cigarette ash. I doubted he recognized me after twenty-five years.

I became the scientist and he my lab rat. He was always alone, eyes locked on his feet, only raising his gaze to keep from walking into a wall. I memorized his patterns, watched him retreat to the same safe space every day, carrying his tray to the back of the cafeteria to eat alone. I never saw him speak, an occasional head nod the only acknowledgement of an outside world.

For a while I imagined what I could do to him, the various ways I might end his life. Sometimes the fantasy was brutal, dousing him in lighter fluid and sparking him up like a torch, or something slower, my knee hard on his sternum, his eyes bulging in recognition as I slowly strangled him. Or a shiv pounded into his center as he watched the life leak out of him. But gradually, playing out every violent scenario, the urge to kill subsided, and I remained content just to watch, curious about what made him tick.

When I was in the basement I'd spend my time anticipating his sound, my internal clock resetting to the man's rhythms, the weight of his steps foretelling how the visit might unfold. If he walked angrily, gait heavy and hard, sometimes cursing while he unlocked the door, I knew the day had gone bad and I would pay the price. I'd retreat to the corner, pushing in hard and covering my head, wondering if this might be the time he went too far. Other nights he would sneak in lightly with a soft murmur, intent on using me to fill some other void, offering what he probably assumed was tenderness. Some nights he could be almost childlike, a gentle big brother come to play.

One day I heard from one of the cafeteria workers that he had stage-four lung cancer, a believable diagnosis given the hollow coughs and thick phlegm he was always hacking up. His movements lapsed to half-speed, his complexion the pale hue of the dying. I knew he would soon be moved to hospice to be pumped full of morphine for his final days, a death that seemed unfairly peaceful for a felon of his accomplishments. So I decided to sit down across from him in the cafeteria as he took slow spoonfuls of soup.

He looked up without surprise, anticipating me. "Do you know who I am?" I asked. He nodded slowly, then stared down at his bowl and continued to eat. Up close his shoulders were narrow, a brittle deflated version of the terrifying specter that shoved me and Dennis into that trunk. We sat in silence, the only sound him slurping his soup. Finally he put down the spoon and looked at me as if we were old friends.

"You and me boy, we just never really left that house, did we?"

And I realized he was right. In some crazy way I would always be there, my head pushing into the car's grill, Impala burned into my brain, or lying under that bed, looking into the clouds of my imagination, wondering when I would hear him unlock the door.

("Impala" was previously published in "Heater", in summer 2015)

Possession

By Charlie Hughes

I'm hurrying home this evening, buzzing with anticipation. Forty-two years old and tonight, for the first time in my life, I am going on a date. It's a tragic fact, which should weigh on me. I should be nervous or fretful or paralysed with anxiety, but I couldn't feel finer. Tonight I'll take Celia out for dinner and we'll have a wonderful time. I just know it.

The bus drops me off and I almost skip down the street. But as I arrive at number 52 I stop at the front gate, look up and take it in. For the first time in a long time, I really see the house. What would Celia think? The paint is peeling off the windows and the front garden is packed full of dead, potted plants. There is a rotting garden stool stood under the porch and the glass in the front door has a large crack down the middle. In the windows there are discoloured curtains, which must have been put up in the 1960's. They are pressed up against the glass from the inside.

* * *

At work, the only sign of my domestic circumstances are the piles of papers on and around my desk. Occasionally someone complains about the mess and my manager has a word with me. When this happens I ask Jeanette, my secretary, to clear it all out for me. I'll take a week off work, usually next to a pool in the south of France, and when I come back, people smile knowingly. "There's our Gerry, ready to start another paper mountain."

My auntie Claire and cousin Amanda have never been to visit. In the early years, after Father died, I'd make elaborate excuses for not inviting them round. There were water leaks and building works and all manner of domestic emergencies preventing me from playing host. Eventually they tired of asking and it just became something they accepted.

I live in one of those quiet pockets you occasionally find in South London. Wide residential streets, lined with attractive terraced housing set close to the pavements. The house was spic and span whilst Mother was around. She would nag my father constantly about his collecting. Once (I couldn't have been older than four) I recall her smashing his antique cameras on the tiled kitchen floor.

Father was always a collector of things and took the trouble to share his enthusiasm with me. My earliest memory is of sitting on his knee in the study whilst he carefully painted a blue tunic on a tin soldier. He was a man of varied tastes: Cameras, stamps, toy soldiers, TV memorabilia, even pinned butterflies. Without mother around to throw things away, we were able to go further, both in size and diversity. Books, newspapers, ornaments, model trains, all sorts. I know father isn't here anymore, not in the physical sense, but with his things all around me, his presence remains.

* * *

I can only just get through the front door, but when I finally do, the hallway is severely cramped. There are boxes of pinned butterflies and other bugs piled precariously up to the ceiling. I have tried to secure them against the wall with a series of ropes, but it is not always effective. I can't see the floor anymore because there are so many letters and bills lying about. I struggle with my correspondence.

Once I'm past the stairs and into the kitchen the smell hits me. These days, I usually wrap something around my face when I go in to cook. Filthy dishes and takeaway packets are strewn everywhere. None of the work surfaces are visible, covered, as they are, with the detritus of meals prepared and consumed long ago. The cupboard doors won't shut because they are rammed full with half-used packets of food or pots and pans of every description.

It's not really possible to get into the living room anymore. I had a phase where I was collecting furniture. All sorts of interesting chairs, coffee tables and even a few sofas. Walking past the door, I can hear the scurrying feet of mice who've made their home in there. Their droplets litter the threshold.

I climb the stairs, dodging more piles of books, bills and letters, and get to my bedroom. Amongst all the chaos (this is where most of Father's ornaments are still kept) there is still a space for me put on my clothes and dress myself. I manage to find a passable shirt and give it a good iron. If I had a radio I think I would turn it on and listen to it. There is a lightness in my heart. I can't wait to see Celia.

* * *

Celia started working at our office three months ago, a new admin assistant with the HR Team.

Female attention is not something I'm accustomed to dealing with, but with her, it all comes rather naturally. Her diminutive frame and pleasant, round face are attractive. But it's her friendly demeanor which I find most arresting.

It began with some light hearted chatter in the coffee room, then she started bringing me little treats to go with my afternoon coffee and it developed from there. Somewhere along the line, I decided I must get to know her better.

When I arrived at work this morning, the lift doors were about to close and Celia jumped in. There we were, exchanging pleasantries about the weather and all the time I was thinking about asking my question. I was going to do it right there and then. I'd just steeled myself, when the lift stopped and Jimmy Hemsworth from Finance got in. I was utterly deflated.

Later, Celia went off to the coffee room and I could see she was in there alone. I got up, checking to see if any colleagues were watching, and went after her. She was at a table reading a magazine.

I sat down, wringing my hands as I decided how to begin. "How are you?"

She looked me over. "Better than you Gerry, you're sweating buckets. Are you okay?"

"Of course. It's just a little hot." I ploughed on. "Celia, I wonder if I could make a suggestion?"

"Oh."

"Would you . . . I mean, could we? Might we be able to go out for a meal together? Might that be something you would want to do, with me, I mean?"

Despite everything, the smiles, the little gifts, the hands casually rested on my shoulder, I was suddenly certain I'd made a serious error of judgement. She grimaced and my heart sank.

"Gerry, I thought you were never going to ask."

I was so stunned, I almost forgot to continue the conversation. She looked at me quizzically and I eventually gathered myself. "Are you free tonight?"

* * *

I was eight years old when Father caught me stealing. He'd gone out to a car boot sale in Harlow early that morning and left the house without saying goodbye. I got my own breakfast and took it upstairs so I could keep warm under the duvet. Father didn't believe in central heating and the house could get perishing in the winter months.

As I ate my toast and jam and drank my tea I thought about how I was going to spend my day. I didn't have any friends to play with, so I decided to set up a big war in the living room with all the toy soldiers. I got quite excited about creating a big battle with the thousands of tin soldiers Father kept.

The living room was heavily cluttered with more of Father's collections. There were stacks of newspapers piled all over the place and a huge cache of old postcards he'd recently acquired. The big table was littered with them, but I needed it for my battle. The big table was always the best place for my allied forces.

I decided father wouldn't mind if I put all of the postcards out of the way. So I got a bin bag from the kitchen, swept all the postcards into it and tossed the bag into the corner of the room. Thinking nothing more of them, I set about laying out the soldiers.

Father returned home much earlier than usual. I was in the middle of setting up a regiment on the mantelpiece when I heard the front door open. I knew something was wrong as soon as I saw his face. He had the same pinched, hateful look the day mother had smashed his cameras.

"What's this?" He asked, gesturing to the bag in the corner of the room.

"The postcards. I just needed them out of the way so I could play with my soldiers."

"You, you were going to throw them out, weren't you?" He was stuttering his words and his hands were shaking.

"No Father. No. I just wanted to play on the..." before I could finish he was on me, fists raining down on my body and head. I curled up and prayed for it to stop but Father had lost all control. As he hit me, he said the same words over and over again.

"You've made a big mistake Gerald. You made a big mistake."

At some point he must have knocked me unconscious because when I awoke I was no longer in the living room, but in complete darkness and freezing. Underneath me I could feel plastic sheeting and irregular lumps of ice. The cold was so intense I could hardly move. When I tried to push myself up my head cracked against a frosty metallic surface.

I screamed as loud as I could, but my voice tiny and pathetic. It was only when Father spoke that I finally realised where I was.

"Cold in there is it Gerry?"

The freezer in the basement. Panic hit me fast.

"Father... Let me out. I'm cold. Please let me out."

"You were going to throw out my postcards, weren't you?"

"No, I promise I wasn't. I'd never do that."

"I've got to be sure, Gerald. I've got to be really sure. I can't have my only son stealing my things away now can I?"

"No. I promise I never will. I'm soooo cold. Please let me out. I'm scared."

"You know what I do with people who steal my things don't you?"

"You make them pay Dad, you make them pay. You told me before. Please, I need to get out. It's hurting too much. I can't breathe."

"That's right. I make them pay. If I forgive you for this boy, if I let you out, I need you to know, next time I'll lock this lid tight and never come back. Do you understand?"

I was sobbing uncontrollably. "Yes. Yes. I understand."

The lid opened and I gasped in the warm, clean air. I wrapped my arms gratefully around his neck and he pulled me out. As I pressed my head against his chest I opened my eyes for just a moment and looked back into the freezer. Beneath a translucent plastic sheeting with ice packed around her, mother's eyes stared back at me.

* * *

The food is wonderful, the wine is excellent and the conversation flows like we've known each other for years. I chose Luccazzi's with care. It is far enough away from home so I wouldn't be recognised, but not so far that, should the evening go well, Celia and I would have the option of returning to my place for a night cap.

She has told me so much about herself tonight. Her family are loving, but a little over protective. She has a dog called Douglas, sometimes paints in her spare time, and is looking for someone to settle down with. Celia said she was interested in me because I seemed different. According to her, there is something of the old-fashioned gentleman to me.

There was a tricky moment earlier when she said she thought I "could do with a bit of spit and polish", adding my appearance was "nothing that a good woman couldn't put right." She seemed to think this was a very funny but I was taken aback. I'm wearing my best green shirt and my chino trousers and I had thought I looked rather smart. I think she noticed my reaction because she put her hand on mine and said, "Don't listen to me. You look lovely Gerry."

Now the meal is over and the restaurant is starting to empty out, we are coming to the point when decisions need to be made. Surprisingly, matters are somewhat taken out of my hands when Celia stands up to go to the ladies. She leans across the table and whispers in my ear. "Let's go back to your place, shall we?" The look she gives me as she walks around the table is something to behold. She wants me.

We hail a cab and I ask to be dropped off three blocks from my house, telling Celia I need a little night air to clear my head. She holds my arm as we walk, at one stage tilting her head and resting it on my shoulder.

Out of the corner of my eye I'm tracking the numbers as we pass.

Thirty, thirty-two, thirty-four. As we near number fifty-two anxiety rises through my body. I still don't know what I'm going to do. I've enjoyed the evening so much and I don't want it to end in any unpleasantness, but what am I supposed to do? I feel trapped.

"Celia." I take my arm from around her and stand in her path.

"Are you angling for a kiss? We can do that inside you know."

"No. It's just there's something I need to explain. Something about my house."

"Really?"

Fidgeting, nervous, I absent-mindedly put my hand into my coat pocket and find something there. Something with a leather grip. Something hard. I think I know what it is but I have no memory of putting it there, nor how it came into my possession. Inside my pocket, I take it in my hand and squeeze the grip, hard. The sensation is familiar, reassuring.

I look into her eyes one more time and try to find the kindness that was there before. It isn't. It never is. She wants to take Father's things, I can see that now.

"Nothing. It's just a little messy. I didn't want you to think I was a slob."

"You had me worried for a minute! Don't be silly. You should see the dive I live in. Come on. Let's go in."

We walk the few extra steps to my home and she doesn't even flinch when we go through the gate. She's looking at me, still holding my arm.

"Well," I say, "here it is. My little castle."

She giggles.

"You go first." I usher her forwards and reach around her to unlock the door. As she steps in her hand reaches up and turns on the light.

She reacts immediately. "Dear God. What the . . ?"

Before she can even start to turn around I take the cosh out of my pocket, raise it high and slam it down onto her head.

Without missing a beat, I'm in through the door and dragging her into the hallway towards the basement.

She can sleep with Mother tonight.

Doing Time On A Pebble

By Paul Stansbury

Guy strode up the hill away from the city with his trainee in tow, the bus stop just visible in the intense light of the street lamps. "This is Pickup where we pick up pickups," he said, once again to his trainee.

"Uh-huh," came the same response.

Their feet made soft scrunching sounds as they plodded along the gravel path. Guy studied the ground at his feet. "I don't know why Top didn't bother to pave the way up here. Almost everything else is paved. But it is not for us to question. Top's motives are mysterious and not necessarily meant to be understood by us." They arrived at the edge of a parking lot under a cluster of street lamps glaring down on the flaking concrete parking lot and some peeling benches. Guy's white Panama suit reflected the light, which filtered down so it seemed almost to glow.

A spindly green creature with a bulbous head was perched on the nearest bench. "That's Pete," Guy said, pointing toward the bench. "He's a Pathfinder like me. He looks like a Pedathian because he picks up Pedathians. I call him Pete for your sake. No one but Pathfinders can understand Pathfinder-speak. And no one but Pathfinders can comprehend Pathfinder names. So we don't even try to tell Pickups our names. Besides, Pete speaks only Pedathian while on duty and since Pathfinders are always on duty, that is all you would hear from him. For the most part, the Pedathian language is unintelligible to humans; not to mention quite harsh on the ears, so don't bother to try to strike up a conversation. Just nod and go on about your business. Like I said, he's here for Pickups like we are." The trainee nodded to the creature, who acknowledged with a circular dip of its head.

Just outside the arc of light, an impenetrable barrier of black loomed. Guy tilted his head slightly, turning an ear toward the black. "Here comes the bus now," he said matter-of-factly, as the growl of an old engine drifted into the light. On cue, an old Bluebird school bus emerged from the misty darkness and ground to a halt, brakes squealing in pain, dragging a storm of blue exhaust. The perfume of partially oxidized hydrocarbons soaked the atmosphere. The bus was painted like a Mexican flag: red on top, a white swath from front to back across its midsection, and green, fading into dust, along the bottom. As the door creaked open, amber-hued interior lights flickered on, leaking through grimy windows wet with the perspiration of the passengers.

A Pedathian driver, resplendent with a tattered generalissimo cap, reminiscent of a South American dictator, hopped out of the door with a fistful of papers, and let out a terrible screak that sounded like the hull of a sinking ship tearing apart.

"Hold fast," Guy muttered, putting his hand on the trainee's arm, "Pete was here before us, so he goes first. Let's hope he's only got one." He had explained this protocol to the trainee time after time during pick ups, but trainees required constant instruction so one more was in order.

Pete tumbled off the bench and ambled up to the driver who stuffed the papers into his outstretched hand. Pete perused the documents and let out his own rendition of a sinking ship. When Pete finished, the driver snapped his spidery fingers. A bulbous green head appeared at the bus door, followed by a gawky set of arms and legs all connected at the center by what resembled a spoonful of green school lunch jello. Pete took his Pedathian Pickup by the hand and set off down the gravel path toward town, his voice tearing metal in a low tone while they walked.

The driver jumped back on the bus. He had barely cleared the door when a Human driver appeared, donning the same grimy dictator cap, and jumped out of the opening. "Got two," he yelled, holding up some more papers and looking about as if he was hailing a transport client at a busy airport.

"Come on," Guy said, grabbing the trainee's arm and moving toward the driver with outstretched hand, "unless you intend to wait for the next bus." He took the papers from the driver and examined them closely. He handed half the documents to his trainee. "These are Transit Authorizations," he said. The trainee furrowed his brow and peered at the papers. "And these are Pickup Assignments," he added shoving the remaining documents into the trainee's hand. "Can't pick 'em up without these papers. Number one of many number one rules passed down from Top. If you forget any rule, don't forget this one." Guy waited as always while the trainee read through the information. "Any questions?"

"Uh-uh," came the usual reply.

"It's highly unusual to have two pick ups."

"Uh-huh."

"Yes, really. You sure you don't have any questions?"

"Uh-uh."

"I'm finished examining the papers. Are you?"

"Uh-huh."

Guy proclaimed at the top of his voice, "Pickups may now depart!" He raised his eyebrow and gave a look at the driver who snapped his fingers. A bewildered looking man with thinning grey hair stepped out from the bus. He looked around, blinking his eyes as they adjusted to the bright street lamps. After he quit blinking, Guy beckoned to the Pickup. "Welcome to Petrogehenna, Pickup. We will take you to your assignment momentarily. Please stand over here by me until the other Pickup disembarks." While the Pickup took up his position, Guy spoke to the trainee. "Got to say the welcome part just like that every time or else Top gets irritated. And you don't want Top to get irritated." He had told this to the trainee every time they welcomed a Pickup, but trainee Penitents had to be constantly trained - it was their assignment.

The driver snapped his fingers once again. Another head, with flowing red hair, popped out of the door. This head, perched on top of a slender female torso, climbed down the steps and stood in front of the others. Guy took a quick look at the papers in his hand and announced, "Welcome to Petrogehenna, Pickup. Says here you are assigned to the task of bus driver. You may now put on the driver's hat." The bus driver handed over the generalissimo hat to the Pickup, who promptly placed it on her own head. A tug on the bill nestled it firmly around its new owner's temples. She hopped up the bus steps, disappearing into its recesses. The door slapped shut, the engine growled, followed by the sound of well worn gears grinding. The bus lurched once, then lumbered off in a cloud of blue exhaust.

"Well, another Penitent begins her tour of duty," Guy said, producing a quill from his shirt pocket and making a notation on one of the papers. "Pay attention," he said to his trainee, "documentation is one of Top's pet peeves. As I said before, number one rule of many number one rules passed down from Top. If you forget any rule, don't forget this one. Comprende?"

"Uh-huh."

"I bet," Guy muttered as he turned his attention to the former driver. "Greetings Parolee, we will take you to Parcels and as soon as your package arrives, you will go to Purge and then to Port." Guy leaned in close his trainee. "Top has a thing about alliteration. Don't ask me why, Top's motives are often mysterious and never to be questioned – in public anyway. Just ask the Bright One. As for Pickups, as soon as they arrive, they already know everything they need to know with regard to how to perform their assigned task. You, as a trainee, know everything there is to know about knowing nothing about the job for which you are training. It's what distinguishes you as a trainee. Make sense?"

"Uh-huh."

"Of course it does. Anyway, like any other trainee, you must be constantly trained by your trainer - that being me - in your immediate activity regarding the job for which I am training you. Unfortunately, you retain nothing as trainees are wont to do, and because you will never be anything other than a trainee during your stay here on Petrogehenna, you require constant retraining."

"Uh-huh."

"Alright then, first stop will be Pizzeria so our Penitent may begin his duties. Then on to Parcels and so on and so on. Follow me." Guy started off down the gravel path which led to Petropolis. The group passed from the glaring lights of Pickup onto the dimmer path. Fewer lights lined the path. Ahead, the buildings of Petropolis looked like stacks of glowing sugar cubes on a black velvet carpet. After they walked a bit further, Guy raised his hand to halt the procession. He looked up to the jet black sky, filled with stars. "Mind you, it's not nighttime here on Petrogehenna. This lonely little rock meanderers through the cosmos without the benefit of a sun to tug it around and shower it with warm radiance. The light here is artificial, courtesy of Top. Breathing gasses are also kindly provided by the Big Guy. No need to thank him, it's all included in the fare. Once in Petropolis, you won't be able to see the stars, so take a look while you can."

He started off once again down the path. The procession continued in its descent until the gravel morphed into a concrete sidewalk which was soon paralleled by a paved street. As they continued toward the city, the road leveled and the distance between the street lamps decreased. They began to pass the sugar cube buildings they had seen from Pickup. All had rows of windows pouring out light. Whatever the height of a building, its attenuate street lamp, festooned with clusters of lights, stretched up to its summit. The group came to an intersection. Guy stopped, raised his hand again, letting out a loud whistle. A dingy, grey cab immediately pulled up, tires screeching as it came to a stop. The cabbie, resplendent with a garish Hawaiian shirt, jumped out, trotted around to the curb and opened the rear door. A woman slid out and stepped aside, raising her hand to hail a cab. "Alright everyone, get in," Guy said, gesturing to the open door, "Next stop, Pizzeria." His trainee, the Parolee and the Penitent climbed into the back seat. Once the Penitent's backside disappeared into the opening, the cabbie slammed the door shut, pirouetted to the front door, opening it with a grand flourish. "Thank you," Guy said, as he took his seat. The cabbie trotted back around, slipped into the driver's seat and sped off. Guy looked over his shoulder at his trainee. "As I have told you before, no need to tell him the destination – cab driver Penitents always know where to go."

The cab dashed through the streets as they journeyed deeper into the heart of the city. The sidewalks grew crowded with pedestrians of all sizes and shapes. Guy named each species they passed for his trainee. "Pay attention, now, there will be a quiz later. The ones with very long ears that look like wings are Gerenukids and the ones that look like hairballs are Teludrians. Then there are the Miglizaks, recognizable by their prominent scarlet dorsal crest, the Cormorunes, with the bright blue facial spots, not to mention the Belgizoids with their purple gills and of course you recognize the Humans. All are Penitents, everyone

one of them, except for Pathfinders, like me, of course." The cab maneuvered through the crowded streets, dodging service vehicles, and other cabs. "No personal conveyances here," he added, "only working vehicles permitted. You getting all this?"

"Uh-huh."

"Oh good. For a minute, I thought I lost you. Well, it looks like we have arrived." The cab rolled to a stop in front of a Miglizak with her arm raised . The cabbie hurried around to the curb and pulled the door open for Guy to exit. Then, he did the same for his other passengers. The Miglizak got in, careful not to bump her dorsal crest. The cabbie flipped the door shut, hurriedly got back in his cab and sped off.

Guy pulled his trainee close by the shirt collar . "Make a note. That was a cab fare Penitent. They do nothing but ride in cabs. Keeps the cab driver Penitents busy when they aren't transporting Pathfinders." He turned loose of the trainee's shirt. "Here we are at Pizzeria," he said, pointing to the bright green neon sign. "All you can eat all the time, provided of course you are an eating Penitent, in which case, all you do is eat all the time. The place is packed with 'em. But please, no special orders. Just plain cheese on plain dough. The pizza cooking Penitents are pizza cooking all the time." He unfolded the Pickup Assignment he had pulled from his pocket. "Hmmm, just double checking. Nope, not an eating assignment or cooking assignment for you, my friend," he smirked. "Did you pinch a nun or something?" He looked at his trainee. "That's a rhetorical question of course." At that moment, a Human Penitent wearing grease soaked coveralls emerged from Pizzeria. The odor of rancid animal fat rolled over the sidewalk like a sandstorm. Guy turned to the Penitent. "Says here you are assigned to the task of grease pit cleaner. You may now put on the coveralls." The grease trap Penitent pulled the sticky hood from his head, and shimmied out of the gooey, stinking coveralls and handed them over to the Penitent who tugged them on and walked straight through Pizzeria's door, disappearing into its recesses. "Well another Penitent begins his tour of duty." Guy produced a fountain pen from his shirt pocket and made a notation on the Pickup Assignment. "Allow me to iterate once more," he said to the trainee, "documentation is absolutely imperative."

Guy addressed the former grease trap cleaner, "Greetings Parolee, we will take you to Parcels and as soon as your package arrives, you will go to Purge and then to Port." Raising his arm, he whistled. Another dingy cab pulled up. The Belgizoid cabbie, like all the other cabbies, scampered around with his Hawaiian shirt tails flapping, and opened the door to exchange passengers. Once accomplished, he slid behind the wheel and took off, leaving its former occupant at the curb hailing another cab.

The cab raced along the crowded streets between intersections, never failing to stop at each for a red light or stop sign. "Part of the charm of cab rides is the stop and go," Guy chortled. "No express lanes for the masses." The congestion lessened as they moved toward the outskirts of the city. The sugar cube buildings grew smaller and vacant lots intervened along the streets. The choke of sidewalk inhabitants gave way to the occasional pedestrian. Fewer street lamps illuminated the pavement. The cab veered to the right and abruptly stopped in front of a furry Teludrian female with arm raised. "We're here," announced Guy. "Or at least this is where we get out of the cab and start walking. Don't dawdle. I'm sure our well-meant Penitent has places to go, as do we."

The change out of passengers was accomplished in the usual speedy fashion and the cab sped back toward the bright light of Petropolis. Guy ushered the group along the street until the pavement faded into a patch of weeds. Just beyond, the concrete sidewalk dissolved into a gravel foot path. "As if I haven't pointed this out to you before," he said to his trainee, "this is the way to Parcel. That's where Parolees pick up their packages. They can't go to Purge or Port until their packages arrive. Savvy?"

"Uh-huh."

"Well, don't forget it," Guy cautioned, rolling his eyes. They followed the path in the sparse light of a few street lamps until a large grey metal building could be seen ahead. The gravel led right up to a large overhead door. To the left was a bench. To the right was a pneumatic tube station. A canister waited in the opening at the bottom of the vacuum tube. Guy pulled some papers from his vest pocket. "Got to put the paperwork in the thing-a-ma-bob," he said, fumbling with the top of the canister, "and... " he paused while his fingers tugged at the canister. Finally the carrier lid swung open and he stuffed the papers inside. "... make sure everything is buttoned up tight, and send it along." He shoved the canister into the opening, pushing the red button next to station. The door began to ascend, accompanied by the wail of gnashing gears.

Light poured out from the building, empty except for a large section of square sheet metal ductwork dropping down from the ceiling just beyond the raised door. Guy pulled the trainee close, "Never, I repeat - which I have done too many times to count - never go inside until the package comes down." The ductwork shuddered, followed by a "Fshhhhhhhhhhhhhhhhhup," then belched out a backpack the size of a refrigerator. It slammed to the floor, kicking up a cloud of dust. Guy held his arm out as a blockade to his trainee. "Wait, remember, we got two Parolees looking for packages." Another shudder shook the building. A small red tag fell, drifting like an autumn leaf wafting in a cool breeze, from the opening. "OK, all safe now. Let's see what we got," Guy called out as he approached the backpack. Guy examined its packing slip tucked inside a clear plastic sleeve. "This is yours," he said, pointing to the former grease trap cleaner Parolee. "Come on and get it." He looked at the former bus driver while pointing to the red tag, "and that's got to be yours." He picked up the red tag and handed it to the Parolee. "It's still searching for your package. Might be a good omen. Sometimes, the smaller ones are hard to find. Take a seat on the bench till it gets here. We'll catch up with you at Purge."

The former grease trap cleaner hefted the backpack up on his shoulders and set off down the gravel path as Guy took his trainee by the arm and walked back to the pneumatic tube station. The moment they cleared the door, it rolled back down, thumping the concrete. "Remember, you got to wait for the paperwork before you leave. If you leave without the paperwork the whole system gets messed up. The whole system gets messed up, Top gets really upset. You don't want that. Number one of many number one rules - et cetera, et cetera, et cetera, as the king would say. Are we clear on that?"

"Uh-huh."

"I bet you say that to all the Pathfinders."

"Huh?"

"Never mind."

A puff of air escaped from the opening of the tube followed by a "Schwiiiiiiiiiiiiiz - pop." A canister appeared. Guy retrieved it and wrestled the lid open. He pulled the paper out and examined it before returning the canister to its cubby hole. He took a ballpoint from his hip pocket and made a notation on the Purge Authorization. "Paperwork, paperwork, can't say it too many times. Right?"

"Uh-huh."

"Right. Let's get back and hail a cab. Got to get to Purge post haste." He led his trainee down the gravel path. As they reached the pavement, Guy raised his arm, and whistled. A cab pulled up. They traded places with its Cormorune Penitent who promptly raised her hand to hail another cab. Their cab driver made a U-turn, barely avoiding the cab that was barreling down the road to pick her up. They passed the backpack toting Parolee just as they got up to speed. "We've got to get to the other side of town and we don't have time for city traffic. Let's take the express," Guy said to the cabbie, who swerved off the pavement and nosed the cab into the sudsy tunnel of an automated car wash.

They emerged as the last soap bubbles were sloughed away by the gentle spray of the spring rain rinse nozzles. The cabbie, who had not let off the gas while they were in the foamy tunnel, pulled back on the pavement and let the cab roll to a stop just in front of the orange and white barricade at the end of the road. There, a Pathfinder and a Gerenukid were waiting. Guy pulled a pocket watch from his vest and eyed the dial. "Only two minutes and a clean cab to boot. Not bad eh?"

"Uh-huh."

"How you doing, Gertie?" Guy said as they traded places in the cab. The Pathfinder wiggled her long ears. "That's how Gerenukids greet others," he said, as the cab whisked away. "They're off to Port."

Just to the side of the barricade a gravel path led up the small hill in front of them. They followed it to the crest. From its vantage, they could see the path dipping down before rising again and terminating at a gate in the center of an imposing grey wall. They spied the back pack toting Parolee trudging along about midway along the path. "Very good," Guy said, nudging his trainee forward, "we should catch up with him at the gate. Come on, while we walk, we'll spend some time talking about time, which on Petrogehenna is not really time. I mean not time as one would expect. Time here is like an insurance sales pitch, it expands and contracts to fit the confines of the space in which it finds itself. Not bound by the unified field theory or Microsoft operating systems, time is free to ebb and flow or otherwise do what it damn well wants. Why? I suspect Top finds it useful.

"Now, in the case of our erstwhile grease trap cleaner, a journey that took two minutes in Pathfinder time, albeit we took the express, may have taken him a year in Parolee time. None the less, we all end up here together. And, I am confident we will find our former bus driver, who we left at Parcel, waiting for us when we reach the gate. That's just the way it works on this pebble. Think of the pizza eating Penitents sitting back there in Pizzeria eating their plain cheese pizzas constantly for hundreds if not thousands of years in Penitent time for what, to us, was a brief stop. What about the Belgizoid cab rider Penitent sitting in a cab at a stop light for a millennium, listening to a Pedathian cabbie Penitent sink the Titanic while we, in the next cab over, have barely enough time to check our watch before the light changes? Training you seems endless to me, I can't imagine how long it is for you. Well, there's time for me to answer any questions you may have. Anything you want to ask?"

"Uh-uh."

"Time to move on then," Guy said, as they caught up with the back pack toting Parolee. It was not long before the three were standing before a large door. The former bus driver Parolee was sitting on a bench with a small box in his lap. "Told 'ya," Guy quipped, pointing to the package wrapped in Kraft paper, "the small ones always take longer." A pneumatic tube station, reached down from the blackness above alongside the bench. It jittered as a canister appeared, accompanied by a "Schwiiiiiiiiiiiiiiiz - foop." Guy retrieved the paper and pencil contained within and placed the canister back in the tube. Making a notation on the Purge Authorization he reminded his trainee, "Paperwork, paperwork, can't say it too many times. Number one of many number one rules."

"Uh-huh."

"What we've got here is failure to communicate," Guy grumbled, lifting the knocker and rapping it three times against the gate. The door swung inward, revealing a vast courtyard. In the center was small man sitting at a bench. Guy beckoned the Parolees and his trainee to follow him as he entered. When they reached the man at the bench, Guy handed him the Purge Authorizations saying, "Greetings, Purger." He examined each and nodded to Guy, who announced at the top of his voice, "The Purge will begin." He motioned to the Parolee holding the small package to approach the bench. As he did, the Purger snapped his fingers. A Teludrian appeared from the dark recesses of the courtyard. He produced a mortar and pestle from a burlap sack, which he placed on the bench. "That's the Assistant Purger," Guy whispered to his trainee.

"Uh-huh."

The Purger selected a Purge authorization, tore it into shreds and placed them in the mortar. Then he nodded to the Parolee with the small package who placed it on the bench and opened it. From within, the Parolee extracted a brown wafer which he held to his forehead before handing it to the Purger, who in turn dropped it into the mortar, then hefted the pestle and began to grind. The Parolee retrieved another wafer, holding it to his forehead before handing it over. Like the one before it, the wafer was placed in the mortar while the grinding continued. Another wafer was produced. It too went into the mixture. While the process continued, Guy pulled his trainee aside. "The wafers are the distillation of all that comprised the Parolee's life before he got here: the good, the bad and everything between. All that was processed into those wafers while he performed his Penitent task. The more there is to purge, the longer the task and in like fashion, the larger the load. Now, the Parolee acknowledges his life by placing the wafers to his forehead, then divests himself of his past by giving them up to the

Purger. Voilà, he becomes ready for Passage." The Parolee handed the last wafer to the Purger who tossed it in the mortar. After a few grinds, he placed the pestle on the table and held out his hand. The Teludrian Assistant retrieved a slender tube from the sack and handed it over. The Purger filled it with the contents of the mortar, holding it out for the Assistant, who took it and backed off into the shadows.

The Purger nodded to the other Parolee who stepped forward, placed his back pack on the bench and opened it, beginning the process again. The Parolee retrieved wafer after wafer from the backpack, holding each in turn to his forehead before handing it over. Just as the Parolee presented his last wafer, the Assistant Purger returned from the shadows, producing another slender tube. As before, the Assistant took the filled tube and disappeared.

"Only one thing left to be done," Guy said to his trainee. "By now he has installed all the necessary pyrotechnic accouterments. Three, two, one . . ." A fat streak of fine sparks shot skyward accompanied by a soft "Phtssssssssssssssssssssssssssss," followed immediately by a twin. The initial trail sparks blinked out, soon followed by the other.

"Wait on it, wait on it," Guy advised. A brilliant flash, followed by a loud bang, broke the silence. High above, petals of glowing embers shot out, filling the sky with a fiery chrysanthemum. A second report, louder than the first, splayed another burning flower above their heads. "Now it's stardust."

By the time the last glowing fragments of the sky flowers had faded, the Assistant Purger had returned to collect the empty box and backpack as well as the contents of his burlap sack. Guy continued to look skyward until two papers drifted down through the night sky. He caught each before they reached the ground. "Always remember to get the Letters of Transit," he said to his trainee, "or it is all for naught." He examined the documents before handing them over to the Purger. "If you don't mind, you fill in the names. That'll make it even more official." The man pulled an inkwell and dip pen from under the bench and proceeded to sign the papers. He handed them back to Guy, who folded them carefully, tucking them into his pocket. "All in order," he said to his trainee, "documentation, number one rule, yada, yada, yada." Then he addressed the two Parolees, "Greetings Passengers, we will take you to Port. Now we really need to get moving, we just have time enough to make the next cab." He nodded to the Purger and led the entourage out of the courtyard and onto the gravel path. Along the way back to the pavement, they met a Miglizak pulling an oxcart heaped full of wafers.

Just as they arrived at the barricade, a cab pulled up, all bright and shiny. A Miglizak Pathfinder hopped out. Just before the cabbie closed the door, Guy put his hands together over his head simulating the Miglizak's crest and called out to the Pathfinder, "He's on the path. Remind me to ask you when I see you next time what he did to deserve an oxcart. Got to run, T-T-F-N." Guy settled in his seat as the cabbie turned onto a wide boulevard. "This is the bypass," he said to the Passengers. "No more city traffic for you. Non-stop to Port it is." No sooner had he said it than the cab pulled up in front of a brightly lit pier.

A Pedathian Pathfinder was waiting. He jumped in the cab as soon as Guy and his group were clear and the cab sped off. Guy pulled the Letters of Transit from his pocket and handed them to the Passengers. "Passengers, this way please, The Livingston is about to dock." He led them down a long, sparsely lit wooden pier. They reached its end just as a small boat, powered by a huffing steam engine, glided into view from the black that surrounded them. It nudged gently into the bumpers that lined the pier. Guy reached into his pocket and handed each Passenger a gold coin. "Give this to Charlie. He'll take good care of you." He turned to his trainee. "Don't forget the coins. Charlie gets crabby if he doesn't get his coins. When Charlie gets crabby, Top gets upset. You get the picture."

"Uh-huh."

Guy held the bow line while the Passengers boarded. "Next stop, Paradise," he called out, shoving the boat away from the dock with his foot. The boat surged forward, its boiler spewing out a cloud of steam and disappeared into the black. "They don't all come through here, ya' know. No matter what their planet of origin, the Dearly Departed have only three ways to move on. Some fly non-stop to Paradise. The majority, though, have to take the bus, with a layover here for adjustment. Then, there are a few deserving miscreants who ride a dung cart, but it ain't to Paradise. Come on," he said, tugging his trainee's arm, "we're due at Pickup."

"Uh-huh."

The Wheel Of Misfortune

By P.J. Sambeaux

Adam nervously fixed his tie in the green room mirror, trying to keep his legs from shaking and his lunch from coming back up. He caught Ínez out of the corner of his eye, glaring at him. He had gone for the 'cute office guy' look as recommended by one of the producers. Ínez had gone for a rustic look: homemade dress, which had been skillfully rolled in mud, and bare feet. They had spent an hour in hair and makeup giving her what the stylist called a 'dusty pueblo" look.

One of the production assistants, a perky red head with freckles, poked her head in the room.

"Ok guys – you're on in five minutes!" She started to leave before remembering something and pulled a bag out of her back pocket. "Oh, Ínez, here are the flies you wanted to swat out of your face."

"Are you fucking kidding me?" Adam cried out, exasperated. He had barely slept a wink since returning from Haiti, and fatigue had eaten away at his normally lovely, upper middle class manners.

Ínez gave him a challenging look, then whipped up her skirt and urinated on the floor.

If her actions were meant to psych Adam out, it worked. He nervously bounced up and down on the balls of his feet. How was he supposed to compete with someone swatting flies out of her face? Urinating on the floor? What was that even? Was it entertaining? More so than pirates? He muttered 'fuck me' under his breath and kicked the garbage can across the room in sheer frustration.

* * *

Colored lights flashed all over the set as the theme song blared and the cameras panned over the contestants. The host casually strolled out and the audience roared.

"Welcome to another round of The Wheel of Misfortune. I am your host, Chip Newton. Before we give that wheel a spin, we're going to have our testimonial round. It will be up to our studio audience to decide which contestants move on to the next round, and which is eliminated. Now contestant one is Destinee from Fort Wayne, Indiana," he began and then paused, waiting for the audience to finish clapping. He wore a golden jacket that was so dazzling it made your eyes water to look at it up close. "Destinee, it says here you regularly get beatings from your alcoholic husband, Dave?"

"I do," Destinee said. The producers had cast her as a modest, yet deserving young woman with a librarian-sort of look.

"And you're currently living in a women's shelter?"

"I am."

"Did they give you the clothes you're wearing?"

"They did."

"How about the underwear you've got on right now?"

"They did."

"And are you allowed to give a shout out to the women's shelter?"

"We're not allowed to let anyone know where we're living, no."

Chip smiled cheekily.

"Well, I promise I won't say it's the Women's Cooperative on Sloane Street."

He threw up his hands like 'whoops' and the producers added the appropriate 'wah-wah' sound effect.

"And actually there's somebody in the audience for you today," he added with a naughty smile. "Dave, can you stand up and wave please?"

"Oh, my god," Destinee gasped, hand over her mouth and her eyes wide with fear as her husband waived at her.

"I'm bad, I know," Chip said directly to camera and threw his arms up to the audience in mock surrender. "Now tell the studio audience why you should move on to the next round."

"I'm a pretty good karaoke singer, and I love drinking and dancing," she said meekly.

Chip nodded his head and shrugged his shoulders as if to say 'not bad.'

"Now our second contestant is Ínez from Santiago, Chile. Ínez, I understand you were a victim of the recent devastating earthquake?"

"Yes, I lost most of my family. My husband broke his back and is crippled for life. So, I have to feed my remaining family of nine by weaving baskets and selling them on the roadside."

"You realize that no one in our audience feels sorry for you?"

"I do. Yes," she said nonchalantly.

"And that no one is pulling for you."

"Yes."

"And if you win, they'll probably burn down that hut you've been living in and run you out of your barrio?"

"Yes."

Adam shuffled in uncomfortably in place. Ínez had obviously practiced for hours at keeping the desperation out of her voice — something he, himself, had not taken the time to do.

"And why should this audience give a damn about Ínez from earthquake devastated Chile?" Chip asked in a booming voice, whipping the viewers in a frenzy.

"I just got a puppy," she answered brightly

The audience oohed and ahhed and Chip nodded his head and clapped in open approval.

Adam clenched his jaw. You can't feed your enormous family, but you could afford a puppy, you fucking liar. He was strictly forbidden under penalty of death from commenting during another contestant's testimonial, so he kept his thoughts to himself.

Chip turned to him next.

"Now our third contestant, Adam, is a disaster relief worker from Houston, Texas. Tell me Adam, do you think you're better than other people?"

"Maybe?" Adam replied and shrugged, not sure of the right answer. "Morally, maybe?"

"It says here you recently went to Haiti. Now was that fun?"

"Well, we were a part of a team dispatched to deal with the cholera epidemic that is decimating their population due to their medieval sanitation system and lack of access to clean water."

"You know nobody cares?"

"I do," he answered, attempting to sound nonchalant, but somehow coming out slightly judgey. He kicked himself – the audience would not miss that.

"And what was Haitian food like? I've always wanted to try, but I'm not quite sure exactly what it is." Chip said with a comically quizzical look, index finger on his lips.

The audience laughed as the prompter indicated for them to do so.

"Well, I actually contracted cholera myself, so I didn't get a chance to sample the local cuisine."

"It's hot in Haiti, right? I bet having that fever helped?"

"No?" Adam replied, again not sure of the correct answer.

"I understand that you had a little surprise on your way home?"

"Yes, our boat was captured by Haitian pirates and my wife was abducted."

"How do you know she's still alive?"

"I got a ransom demand in the mail, a very high ransom demand I can't even begin to pay with my salary..."

"How do you know it's not a hoax?" Chip interrupted.

"Um, one of her fingers came with the demand," Adam said, the pitch of his voice climbing as he attempted, but failed, to sound unconcerned.

"How do you know it was *her* finger?"

Adam sighed deeply.

"It was wearing her wedding ring."

"Ouch!" Chip turned to the studio executioner. "Now Shaza, how many fingers do you think you've chopped off in your career?"

Shaza shook his head. He was a burly man with a thick, muscular neck bulging out from the collar of his military uniform.

"Too many to count," he said and chuckled.

"Adam, why should the studio audience send you to the next round?"

Adam knew he should say something fun, something entertaining – the producers had even coached him on being fresh and irreverent – but he just didn't have it in him. Instead he mumbled 'my wife' lamely, his eyes glued to the floor.

Chip rolled his eyes, and a chorus of trumpets rang out to indicate the end of the testimonial round.

"Now we all know what time it is," Chip began, spinning toward the camera in a practiced way. "For those of you at home who are joining us for the first time, the studio audience is about to vote on which contestant to eliminate. And," he added, pausing to adjust his collar comically, "I'm pretty sure it's not going to be the lady who got a puppy."

The audience laughed and gave an appreciative clap. He winked and pointed at them, which, mysteriously, made them clap harder.

Everyone watched as the tabulations of the audience votes were projected on the big screen. They played special chilling music with sound effects that built to a crescendo as the final votes came in and the screen lit up.

"Ok, the audience has locked in their final vote," Chip announced, waiting for the name to appear. "And the loser is...cholera Adam!"

Adam panicked and started to run – they all did at this point in the show – but three guards cornered him. They did a comedy sketch where an inexperienced guard tried to shoot him, but then realized his gun wasn't loaded. The audience laughed without even being prompted.

This is how it ends, Adam thought, this is all perfectly logical: You try to help a less fortunate nation. You get the disease you're trying to fight. You get boarded by pirates less than a mile from shore. Your wife, who your mother says rigged the whole thing because she was sick both of you and of humanitarian aid work, gets abducted. You lose everything on a game show trying to win the ransom money to get her back, because you're not entertaining enough, and then they shoot you. It's all part of the circle of life. The absurdity of it all made him giggle. The more experienced officer in the skit took aim and shot him dead as a doornail. They dragged his body away, leaving a bloody trail on the linoleum floor, which the studio cameras did a close up on.

"We have a bonus dismemberment hiding somewhere this next round – and you know we have our own Shaza the executioner, direct from Chop Chop Square in Central Command to take care of that for us," Chip said brightly, not missing a beat.

Here Shaza nodded and gave a friendly wave to the camera. The frat boys in the audience stood and did a special grunting cheer for him, followed by the chop chop dance, which Shaza did back in return.

Chip flashed a toothy smile directly into the camera.

"So let's give that wheel a spin!"

Let Zombies Live, As It Were

By Daniel LaPonsie

It was colder than the back-side of Frosty the Snowman's nuts, and yet my delivery van still stunk from three weeks' worth of corpses. So I think I could be forgiven for being anxious to get to Detroit, to escape the aroma of rot, stale sweat, and piss. That's why my eyes were continuously glancing at the time, counting the hours and minutes. That, and the fact that she'd be waking up soon, as they do.

The drumbeat of horrific luck that had plagued me that week had been nothing if not consistent. A new Homeland Security checkpoint had sprung up between me and my destination, caught me by surprise. Not "surprise" in the sense of friends leaping out from behind your living room furniture with balloons and gifts. No, it was more like a sudden boil arriving over one eye. Or the onset of incontinence in the middle of intercourse.

Fiona Apple was crooning away on my radio. Outside, the cold night air was shot through with a dozen spotlights. Eventually, a single officer stepped out of the booth, gut dangling below an ill-fitting winter coat, and crossed the icy highway toward my idling van. Fatty's flashlight bounced in rhythm to the current track, "Criminal." It struck me as funny to watch the portly TSA officer swagger up to my delivery van accompanied by the seductive beat of the song, gut swinging like a pendulum. "Let me know the way, before there's hell to pay. Give me room to lay the law and let me go …"

I let the officer rap on my window with the end of his flashlight before turning the radio off. Couldn't roll the window down, it was frozen shut. Stupid heater. So I opened the door, and a blob of snow plopped into my lap. I uttered an expletive, and then flashed my best smile at all three-hundred pounds of doughnut oil and lonely nights standing next to me. "Help you, officer?"

Expressionless, he swept a flashlight beam from me to a stack of thick red envelopes on the passenger seat, to my lunchbox, and then back across the dash. He paused at a photo of my little girl taped to the dash – red hair in pig-tails, her missing tooth prominently displayed. Daisy had a relentless smile.

"Just turned ten," I said.

The officer aimed the light back at me. "Papers please."

You know that isn't your daddy's United States of freaking America when men with guns go around asking for "papers please."

"Right here officer."

"What's your business in Toledo this time of night? You aware of the curfew?"

"I'm on my way to Detroit, officer. I deliver bodies to Our Lady of Good Intentions. Government research, looking for a cure."

The officer's eyes widened. "Bodies?"

"Well, only one body tonight, officer." Gave him my business card. You never know when you might stumble upon a potential customer. "Yes, sir. But that's not all I deliver. Reginald Smiley's Speedy Delivery Service, as it says on the side of my van." I flashed my smile again. Felt like I had to – it's in the name. "Been in business for myself for a year. Just me, as I said. Well, me and my daughter, actually. But she's only ten, as I told you."

The officer stumbled backward, eyes wider than Orson Welles's backside. He nodded furiously and waved at me to shut up. "I'm sure everything is in order. Just get that thing outta here, quick as you can. Understand?" He pulled out a handkerchief, put it over his mouth.

"She's in the back, if you want to meet her," I offered, but he was already gone.

I watched as he scurried a few feet from the van, slipped and fell on his ass, got back to his feet and hustled toward the guard booth. The barricade was raised within seconds. Soon as I was on the other side of the checkpoint, I was elated. Only sixty more miles to Detroit. I quickly flipped the Fiona Apple cassette over to side B. Ya, cassette. Old school. That's how I roll. And I couldn't help but to drum my hands on the cold steering wheel while peering through the eight-inch clear spot on the windshield.

The reason I was feeling so jazzed was pretty simple: I was gonna be King Hell. Kid A. Finally, I was on my way to realizing a sense of purpose.

Gonna be somebody important. After forty-seven years of misery, a litany of failures, the gods were finally on my side. Could almost feel an otherworldly tentacle on my shoulder. I'll tell you what, my wife wouldn't have left me if she could see me now.

Well, I'm kidding myself. She would have left me much faster.

"Sixty miles, Sweetie," I said over my shoulder. "Almost there." My words fell on deaf ears.

* * *

Dark and cold and really damn lonely. That's how I would describe the next thirty miles. I'd made this trip several times in recent weeks, carrying the recently bitten from Cleveland Memorial to Our Lady. The pay's been ok. But I didn't recall the journey taking this long.

I couldn't stop shivering. After listening to the same cassette over and over again, I shut it off and began to hum to myself. Anything to keep my mind active and to pass the time. Would have been nice to have a working radio – all I could get from the dial was static. Must have passed at least fifty military outposts already. Passed a good hundred used-to-be-zombies, too. The former "living dead" were littering the shoulder of the highway, heads either blasted off or caved in.

Came across one who was laying just far enough into the lane that I ran over it. It was totally an accident – pretty sure it had been moving. Did my best to avoid it, I really did. My heart broke as it's head exploded against my front bumper, lobbing black goop and bits of scalp across the windshield. The whole van shook as the passenger-side tires rolled over the helpless creature. Wanted to yell an apology out the window but it was still frozen shut. Stupid heater.

Not long ago, I had been exactly like the zombie-haters. It's understandable. Like most businesses, Reginald Smiley's Speedy Delivery Service hit a snafu when the so-called zombie apocalypse descended upon us. The infection had taken everyone by surprise, spreading faster than a hooker in Skechers. It's hard to run a business when all your customers are being eaten, or joining the walking dead. Unless you're selling brains.

Hey, that might be something to look into. Always on the lookout for opportunity.

And speaking of opportunity, soon as I heard that a government lab had been set up in a Detroit hospital, and was seeking victims of the plague for research, I was all over that opportunity like tattoos on a biker chick. Boy howdie, I needed the work! Apocalypse or not, I still have a beautiful daughter to look after.

The trips had been a heck of a lot of fun for Daisy. She loved to ride next to me, holding the map, being my little navigator. It had given us something to do, as we waited for the plague to blow over. Seriously, if we lose our grip on family, we lose our grip on our humanity. That's what I always say.

It was on that last trip, which took place on Daisy's birthday, that I had a change of heart about our undead brothers and sisters. While thinking about my newly-found cause, I gripped the rear view mirror and twisted it at an angle so that he could keep an eye on the back of the van. Should have been in Detroit by now. Thought I saw an arm lifting. Just as I looked over my shoulder, the van jerked abruptly. Must have hit a pothole.

The highway was icy, visibility was lousy, and struggling with that steering wheel was tougher than trying to drive it home in an oily three-dollar whore. In other words, the van went all over the road, and finally, despite my best intentions, I plowed it into a snowbank and the engine petered out.

Everything went still, and quiet. It hurt to move my head. And then I could hear Daisy shuffling, moving around in the back of the van. She was awake. Darkness overtook me.

* * *

"Hello? Any body alive in there?" The voice was muffled, coming from behind a wall of snow. When I touched my head, my fingers came away sticky. I reached up and turned on the dome light, saw blood on the steering wheel. How long had I been out? Tried the door, but it wouldn't open.

"Hey, pal. Gimme a hand with the door, would you?"

"You're pretty well stuck in a snowbank," the man said. "I've got a shovel in my car. Be right back."

The sound of shuffling from behind me reminded me that I was out of time. My darling little angel was awake. I tried to force the door with my shoulder. A small hand landed on the back of my seat. Dried birthday cake was still on her fingernails. We had just stopped for dinner, and birthday cake, and celebrated her turning ten. She only ate the frosting, like usual. When she looked over the seat with her dead, grey eyes, I was pleased to see that her pigtails were still in. Her hair gets all frizzy and crazy, unless we put it in braids or pigtails.

She reached toward me. I dodged her hand, slid over to the passenger seat. "Get me outta here!" I tried that door and got similar results, but it felt less stuck than the driver's side door. So I laid back with my feet toward it and gave it a kick. While I'll always love my undead daughter, I was never in a huge hurry to join the walking dead.

"Got a shovel. Hold on." I could hear a metal blade being sharply inserted into the snow just on the other side of the door. I kicked again, felt it give a little. My darling little girl started climbing over the seat back, toward me, mouth agape. No breathing. No sound. She used to be a heck of a chatterbox, and maybe that's what I found so unsettling. I kicked at the door again. And again.

"Hold on, mister."

"I can't hold on." Kicked again.

Her pudgy, cold hand was on my shoulder.

A firm kick, in the center of the door. It flew open. My rescuer fell to his back. I launched myself from the van, scrambled to my feet, and slammed the door shut.

"Jesus, mister. Your van on fire? I didn't see any sign."

Took a minute to catch my breath again. I bent over, hand on my knees, shook my head. "Transporting a subject to Detroit. I'm late. Out of time."

Calling them "subjects" didn't used to bother me. Now the word felt dirty.

"Zombie?"

I nodded my head and looked over to him. My rescuer was a Michigan state trooper. Skinny dude clad in snow pants, and a thick highway patrol jacket. He was pretty young, by the looks of him. But Michigan had been going through cops like maggots through corpses. His patrol car was parked up along the highway.

"Already called a tow-truck, Sir. Might be a while before they get here."

"That's no good, man. I'm already late. And she's awake. Can't drive a van with her tugging at my shirt, changing the radio station and, you know, trying to eat me."

The officer scratched at his stubbly chin, gave me a really queer look. "DARPA just came out with these new tranquilizers. They say just one will put 'em down right away, and keep 'em knocked out for a good thirty minutes." He gestured at his belt. A long chrome gun was visible between the black grip of his pistol and his boxy yellow taser. "I can give it a shot, if you like."

A gust of wind kicked up a swirl of pellet-like snow that pricked at the side of my face. He trudged through the snow toward the back of my van. I picked up his shovel.

"This should only take a moment," he said.

He opened the rear doors of the van, and I saw her sitting in the passenger seat. Waiting, perhaps, to hit the road again? The possibility tugged at my heart strings. She turned, and stared at the officer.

"Has that been tested?" I said. "Is it humane?"

"Excuse me?" he said. He turned toward me, briefly, appearing puzzled at a perfectly respectable question.

"Just asking."

"Sure." He shrugged, and prepared to line up a shot.

She climbed over the back of the seat and landed on the cold metal floor. Her face bore an expression of plaintive hunger. It was then that realized that she hadn't had anything to eat in the last twenty-four hours, aside from a bit of cake frosting.

I stood just behind the officer, shovel in hand. Just as he was squeezing the trigger, I hauled back and brought the shovel down on the top of his head. The officer stood there, rocking back and forth, spitting blood from his mouth. His words came out slurred. "What are you doing?" It was good he was still alive. They seem to prefer 'em still alive.

Daisy continued crawling toward the rear of the van, as I fished his keys from officer's pocket, and fetched his gun. Then I grabbed him by the arms and dragged him to his police cruiser. I'd never seen the back seat of a cop car, and didn't realize that there was so little room back there. Movies and television always make them look like an ordinary back seat. There was actually no foot room, and I had to lay him sprawled out across the seat.

Good thing Daisy was so slow. It gave me time to get the dinner into the back of the cruiser, leave one door open, and then climb into the driver seat. There was a handy divider between the front and back seats. It had a window in the center that you could open if you wanted to have a conversation with the guy in back – which made me think of a confessional. Was that guilt whispering into my ear? Wouldn't be the first time I ignored my conscience. Wouldn't be the last, either.

I turned around and watched the officer groggily trying to figure out was happening, moving his arms around, attempting to shimmy back out of the car. He was slower than my living dead daughter. Soon as she was in, I jumped out and slammed the door behind her.

Aside from the properly working heater, was the benefit of a riot gun nestled between the two front seats. While Zombie Daisy enjoyed her first meal, I went back to the van to fetch the officer's tranquilizer gun, the red envelopes and, oh yes, the fuckton of explosives. I thought to myself, zombie liberty is at hand. I was gonna be Thomas Paine. George Washington. Joan of Ark. I was gonna be freaking V, from that Alan Moore comic book.

* * *

After about five miles, a wrecker flew past us. I presumed it was the one the cop had called for us. Flipped the radio on in time to catch a public service announcement from the Secretary of Homeland Security, Nathan Scabs. His voice was dripping with faux paternal concern as he encouraged neighbors to watch one another. He listed signs of infection to watch for, such as unusually cool body temperature, eyes rolled into the back of the head, sudden craving for human flesh. He further encouraged citizens to report such things to the local authorities. If we do not have the utmost vigilance, Scabs stated, "the zombies win."

It was eerie seeing Detroit in such desolation, although I know full well that the city had been on its downward spiral long before any walking dead started haunting its streets. I slowed down near a post box and saw a gun-happy civilian taking shots at an innocent living-dead brother across the street. Disgusted, I grabbed the riot gun and the red envelopes, and jumped out of the cruiser.

"They still have mail delivery in this town?"

"Sometimes," he said. Then he took a shot at the zombie across the street, only grazed her shoulder.

"Don't do that."

"Don't do what?" He fired again, missed.

With a sigh, I drove the butt of the gun right between the eyes of the zombie-hating turd. He fell flat on his back, stunned, and a swift kick sent his gun spinning across the street. And then I dropped the letters into the mailbox. Dude looked surprised. The zombie came shuffling toward him. A second one came from around the corner – a runner. That one got to him first. I didn't stick around to watch, but I sure hope the runner shared with his slower brother. Selfishness can make monsters of anybody.

The envelopes were all addressed to various news media, and the United Nations. They contained a list of demands that, should they be followed, would amount to human rights being extended to zombie-kind. One thing I included in the list that I was particularly proud of was a demand for zombies to be granted grazing rights in cities that I didn't think would be missed, like Grand Rapids, Michigan.

Other demands included Congressional representation, voting rights, anti-discrimination legislation, and a marriage law permitting living and living-dead unions. After all, true love doesn't discriminate between life and death, so why should we?

Naturally, the letter explains that if the demands aren't taken to heart, other attacks would follow. I assumed that my intended bombing of Our Lady of Good Intentions would inspire like-minded masses to rise up.

I zipped through a yield sign, and came to a rolling stop at a stop sign. The hospital was in sight, several blocks away. I felt my pulse quicken. The next moments were being rehearsed in my mind. I'd pull up to the main entrance of the hospital, climb out of the vehicle, open the rear door, and I'd run off down the street. My zombie daughter would shuffle away to safety. The bomb would explode, removing the entire front of the hospital. The news media would take note of the attack and circulate my demands via radio, television, and print. Like-minded activists would follow my example, and the road to zombie and non-zombie reconciliation would be paved in a confetti of blood and broken glass.

Meanwhile, my daughter would run off to enjoy the natural habitat of her kind: the dank streets of a dead city. She'd be free to romp and graze and live, as it were, with other walking dead. This was my purpose in life: zombie activism! I tossed my head back and laughed. Destiny was a mere three blocks away. Two-and-a-half. Two blocks. I could read the sign from this distance, "Our Lady of Good Intentions: God's Love is the Greatest Salve."

But then I could feel my little darling's fingernails break the skin on my neck. Didn't I latch the window? I wasn't sure how she could have forced it open from the other side, but I supposed it didn't matter. My skin was torn open like a harlot's blouse. As I tried to push her hand back through the window behind me, she managed to bite one of my fingers off at the knuckle.

The scratch on my neck hadn't been enough? It was pretty clear at this point that the gods had withdrawn their tentacles of compassion and goodwill from me, and left me to my former life of failure and mediocrity. It was as apparent as the crimson fluids that were spraying all over the inside of the car.

With my head down, both hands on the back of my neck, and inside of the windshield quickly becoming covered-over in my blood, the car swerved freely across the street until it slammed into a telephone pole. I had gotten close to my destination, for what it's worth. Daisy and I were right across the street from the hospital.

I must have blacked out at that moment, because when my eyes fluttered open, I saw emergency room doors exploding open at my feet. I was taken into the center of an operating room, and a doctor was discussing administering a hoped-for cure.

"This is a godsend. A miracle," one doctor said, pulling a mask over his face. "We needed someone freshly infected. And just such a patient was delivered to our doorstep. Lets see if this cure indeed works."

"We can compare the results between this man and the girl," the other said. "Her infection has clearly progressed well into the third stage."

I attempted to protest, but was too weak. They put me under, and when I came to, I was told that would not be joining the ranks of the walking dead. Abundant success for them. But as I lay on the table, eyes blinded by the unforgiving lights of the examination room, I couldn't shake the feeling that I had suffered another insurmountable failure.

What a let-down! I had just warmed up to the idea that my cold dead ass was gonna stalk the streets alongside my darling Daisy, frolicking along desolate streets. And I was really hoping I'd get to be a runner. That would be totally bad-ass.

Stupid vaccine.

My little girl remains undead. Obviously, the vaccine didn't cure people who'd already completely succumbed to the virus. They had discovered a mere inoculation. Upon release from prison, I was pleased to find that Daisy's foster family had weaned her off human flesh, although she still preferred raw meat and brains. Which reminded me of that excellent business idea I had stumbled upon. I need to jump onto the brains market before other entrepreneurs realize it's a business idea just begging to be exploited.

This is my calling. I'm gonna make a killing on this idea! I'm thinking that my daughter and I can drive around the country picking up transients. She can hold the map. "How about a road trip, Darling?"

("Let Zombies Live, As It Were" was previously published in "Tales of the Zombie War", in March 2013)

Author Biographies

In Order of Appearance

Terrance Gutberlet has published fiction in *Euphony Journal*. He is currently an MFA student at the University of New Orleans. He also teaches at a high school for autistic students.

Michael B. Tager is a writer from Baltimore. He is the author of the fiction collection *"Always Tomorrow"* and *"Pop Culture Poems"*, a poetry chapbook (*Mason Jar Press*). He is currently writing a book of memoir told through essays about video games. He likes Buffy and the Orioles. Find more of his work online at michaelbtager.com.

MK Sauer is the author of *"Star-Crossed"*, a steampunk speculative fiction novel, *"Retriever"*, a sci-fi story published in Luna Station Quarterly, *"Chrysalis"*, a sci-fi, cyberpunk story published by *Devilfish Review*, and *"The Thief In The Sand"*, due to be published by *Stoneskin Press* in the *Cthulhu V. Swords* anthology. She received a degree in Russian Literature from the University of Colorado at Boulder. Her twitter handle is @MK_Sauer.

Mike Crumplar is a recent graduate of the College of William and Mary in Virginia and currently works in Washington, DC as an editor. He blogs at *triggerwave.net* and can be reached on Twitter @mcrumps.

Taryn Hook's writing credits include winning second place in the *Fairbanks Daily News-Miner* short story contest. Her work, *"Pluto Rising"*, was also included in the *Writing Disorder*'s 2011 Anthology of short stories. Ms. Hook's speculative short stories have also appeared in *Hadrosaur Tales, Steel Caves, 69 Flavors of Paranoia, Horrorfind, Malevolence,* and *Zahir*.

Justin Tate grew up in Ada, Oklahoma, and now resides near the Superstition Mountains in Apache Junction, Arizona. He writes scary stories for fun and has been fortunate enough to have his works featured in multiple literary journals, webzines and anthologies. Follow him on social media for updates on new stories and to show your support: Facebook.com/JustinTateAuthor, Twitter: @DeathSonnets.

R.B. Roth lives in Pittsburgh, Pennsylvania. A devout follower of the liberal arts, she nevertheless works for and with scientists. She also volunteers at a local animal shelter.

Jon Michael Kelley's fiction has recently appeared in such literary anthologies as *Qualia Nous* (2014 Bram Stoker Award Finalist for Best Anthology, *Written Backwards Press*); *Chiral Mad 1 & 2*; *Firbolg Publishing*'s most ambitious *Dark Muses, Spoken Silences*; *Triangulations: Lost Voices* by *Parsec Ink*, and *Sensorama* by the UK's *Eibonvale Press*. Jon lives in a gold-mining town in the mountains of Colorado.

Jack Granath is a librarian in Kansas. His website can be found at *www.jackgranath.com.*

Elizabeth Dadabo has only recently embraced winter. She is a lifelong resident of the Chicago area and is thus appropriately fatalistic. She enjoys doing whatever life asks of her.

Since beginning his full-time literary career a year ago, **Timothy O'Leary** has been the winner of the 2015 winner *Aestas Short Story Award*, and a finalist for the 2015 *Mississippi Review* prize, the *Washington Square Review* prize in fiction, and the *Mark Twain* award for humor writing. His essays and short stories have been published or are forthcoming in many magazines and journals, including *Talking River*, *The Fredericksburg Literary Review*, *Pooled Ink*, and the anthologies *And All Our Yesterdays*, and *The Water Holds No Scars*. His non-fiction book, *"Warriors, Workers, Whiners & Weasels"* was published in 2006. He received his MFA from Pacific University, and resides in the Columbia Gorge, near Portland, OR. More information can be found at *timothyolearylit.com*.

Charlie Hughes is a 38 year old writer. He writes crime, suspense and horror fiction. Originally from Leeds, he now lives in London. His story *"Peartree Road"* appears in the *Crooked Holster* anthology, published in December 2015. He recently won the *Bookers Corner* Monthly Writing Competition with his story *"The Letter"* which will also be published in their forthcoming anthology. His stories have also appeared online at *The Cro Magnon* and *SFReader.com*.

Paul Stansbury is a life long native of Kentucky. Now retired, he lives in Danville, Kentucky. He frequently reads his work in public. His poetry has appeared in *Kentucky Monthly*. His stories have appeared in the anthologies, *Brief Grislys*, published by the *Apocryphile Press* and *Neo-Legends To Last A Deathtime* published by *KY Story*. He has a story soon to be published in an anthology by *SEZ Publishing*. His work has also appeared in a variety of on-line publications.

P.J. Sambeaux's work has appeared in such magazines as *Maudlin House*, *Space Squid*, *The Broken City*, *Alliterati*, *Flash Fiction Magazine*, and *The Rain, Party & Disaster Society*. She is currently working on her second novel about a suicidal secretary who is obsessed with Chernobyl. She lives in Pittsburgh.

Daniel LaPonsie lives with his wife and children in Grand Rapids, Michigan. He prefers kittens to puppies, coffee to tea, Linux to Mac, and Star Wars to Star Trek. Daniel can be found at *www.pinkjetpack.com.*

To submit to Issue 3 of Abstract Jam, please visit *www.abstractjam.com.*

Twitter: *@AbstractJam*   General E-mail: *contact@abstractjam.com*

Printed in Great Britain
by Amazon